How to Use This Book

Look for these special features in this book:

SIDEBARS, **CHARTS**, **GRAPHS**, and original **MAPS** expand your understanding of what's being discussed—and also make useful sources for classroom reports.

FAQs answer common **F**requently **A**sked **Q**uestions about people, places, and things.

WOW FACTORS offer "Who knew?" facts to keep you thinking.

TRAVEL GUIDE gives you tips on exploring the state—either in person or right from your chair!

PROJECT ROOM provides fun ideas for school assignments and incredible research projects. Plus, there's a guide to primary sources—what they are and how to cite them.

Please note: All statistics are as up-to-date as possible at the time of publication.

Consultants: William Loren Katz; J. Richard Kyle, University of Texas–Austin; Richard B. McCaslin, Professor, University of North Texas

Book production by The Design Lab

Library of Congress Cataloging-in-Publication Data
Somervill, Barbara A.
 Texas / by Barbara A. Somervill.
     p. cm.—(America the beautiful. Third series)
 Includes bibliographical references and index.
 ISBN-13: 978-0-531-18580-3
 ISBN-10: 0-531-18580-X
 1. Texas—Juvenile literature. I. Title. II. Series.
 F386.3.S66 2008
 976.4—dc22   2007017787

1 2 3 4 5 6 7 8 9 10 R 18 17 16 15 14 13 12 11 10 09

AMERICA ★ THE ★ BEAUTIFUL

Texas

BARBARA A. SOMERVILL

Third Series

Children's Press®
An Imprint of Scholastic Inc.
New York ★ Toronto ★ London ★ Auckland ★ Sydney
Mexico City ★ New Delhi ★ Hong Kong
Danbury, Connecticut

CONTENTS

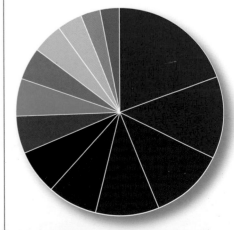

GROWTH AND CHANGE

4

Texas started as an independent country, became a U.S. state, joined the Confederacy, and rejoined the United States. . .

MORE MODERN TIMES

5

Texas survived the Great Depression, enjoyed a rising oil market, and grew into a major economic power.

9 TRAVEL GUIDE

Take in a baseball game, see where famous battles were fought, or enjoy a conjunto band—that's Texas! . . .

PROJECT ROOM

★

COLORADO   KANSAS   MISSOURI

Cadillac
Ranch

Canadian

OKLAHOMA

AMARILLO

NEW MEXICO

ARKANSAS

American Quarter Horse
Heritage Center & Museum

Red

National Cowgirl
Museum and
Hall of Fame

African American
Museum

LUBBOCK

Llano Estacado

FORT WORTH

DALLAS

Caddoan Mounds
State Historic Site

EL PASO   Guadalupe
Mountains

Colorado

Texas Sports
Hall of Fame

Brazos

Trinity

TEXAS

WACO

Sabine

Pecos

Lady Bird Johnson
Wildflower Center

Cockrell
Butterfly
Center

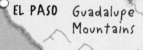

Big Bend
National Park

The Alamo

AUSTIN

MEXICO

Rio Grande

HOUSTON

Texas State Capitol

Lyndon B. Johnson
Space Center

SAN ANTONIO

0   80
Miles

Rio Grande

Nueces

Fort McIntosh

LAREDO

CORPUS
CHRISTI

Aransas National
Wildlife Refuge

Padre Island
National
Seashore

Rio Grande Valley

BROWNSVILLE

GULF OF
MEXICO

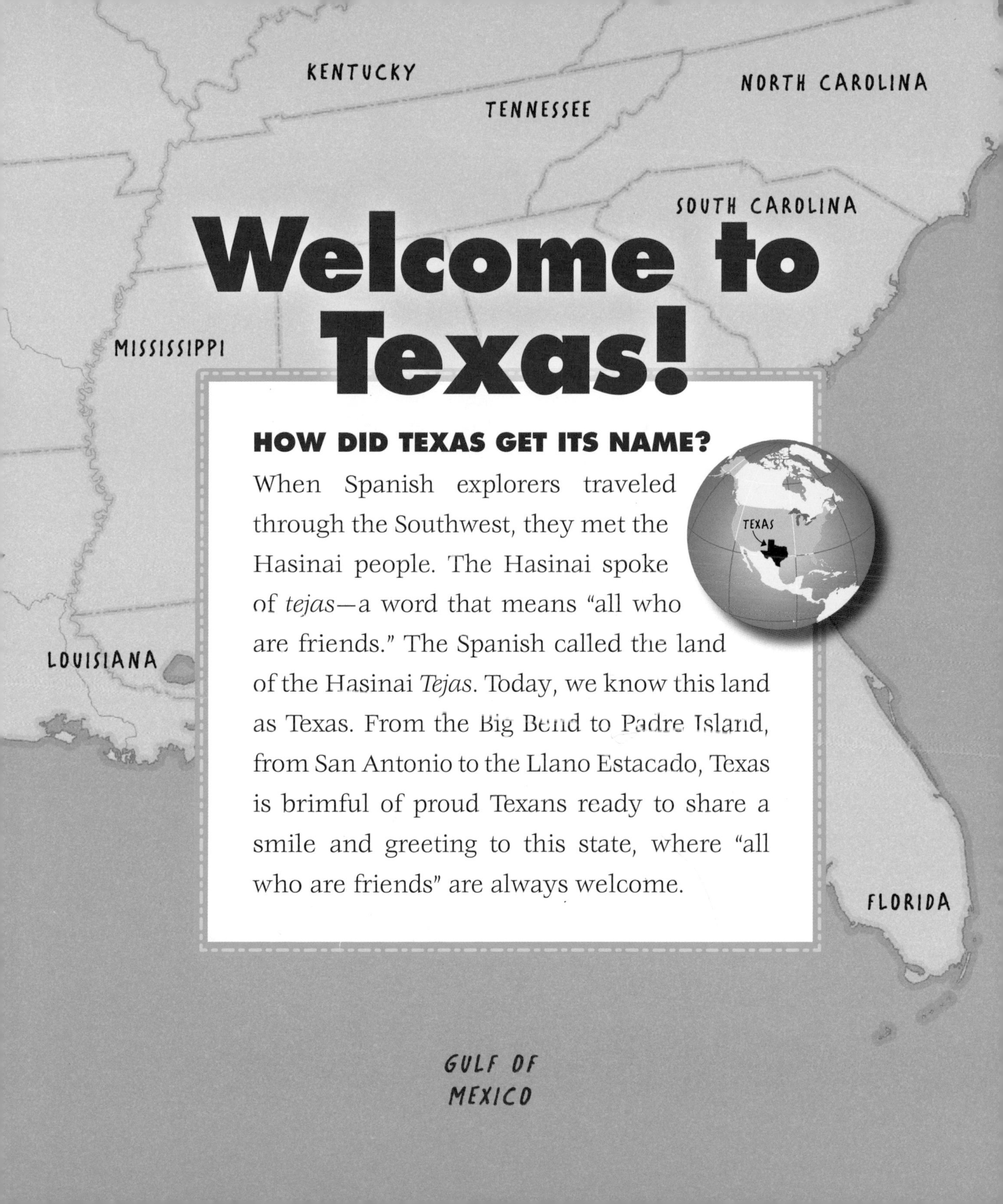

Welcome to Texas!

KENTUCKY

TENNESSEE

NORTH CAROLINA

SOUTH CAROLINA

MISSISSIPPI

LOUISIANA

FLORIDA

HOW DID TEXAS GET ITS NAME?

When Spanish explorers traveled through the Southwest, they met the Hasinai people. The Hasinai spoke of *tejas*—a word that means "all who are friends." The Spanish called the land of the Hasinai *Tejas*. Today, we know this land as Texas. From the Big Bend to Padre Island, from San Antonio to the Llano Estacado, Texas is brimful of proud Texans ready to share a smile and greeting to this state, where "all who are friends" are always welcome.

TEXAS

GULF OF
MEXICO

READ ABOUT

Spring wildflowers
at Caprocks
Canyon State Park

CHAPTER ONE

LAND

★

EVERYTHING'S BIGGER IN TEXAS— AT LEAST, THAT'S WHAT TEXANS SOMETIMES SAY. In fact, Texas itself is big. With 268,581 square miles (695,625 square kilometers), it's the second-largest state in the Union, trailing only Alaska. The state's lowest points lie along the coast, where white sand beaches meet the Gulf of Mexico. Texas has 90 mountains that rise above 1 mile (1.6 km) high, including the tallest, Guadalupe Peak, which rises to 8,749 feet (2,667 meters). Texas's immense size also leaves plenty of room for deserts, dense forests, rolling grasslands, high plateaus, and soggy swamps.

These fossils of sea stars found in Texas date to 85 million years ago.

CHANGING LAND

Over the past 600 million years, the land we know as Texas has undergone dramatic changes. Several times, Texas rested under shallow oceans. When plants and animals in these oceans died, they sank to the bottom. As the years passed, mud, sand, and other **sediment** buried them. This sediment turned into rock, and the plant and animal life beneath it slowly decayed. Over time and under heat and pressure, that decaying matter developed into petroleum, the basis of Texas's multi-billion-dollar oil industry.

More recently—at least in geological time—an ice age brought colder weather. During the ice age, more of the earth's water was frozen into ice, so sea levels were much lower. At this time, the shoreline extended more than 100 miles (160 km) farther into the Gulf of Mexico than it does today. The types of plants changed with the climate, and pine forests emerged in east-

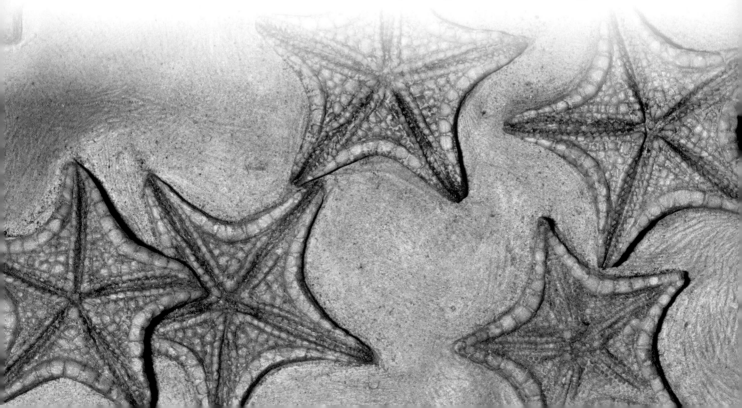

Texas Topography

Use the color-coded elevation chart to see on the map Texas's high points (dark red to orange) and low points (green to dark green). Elevation is measured as the distance above or below sea level.

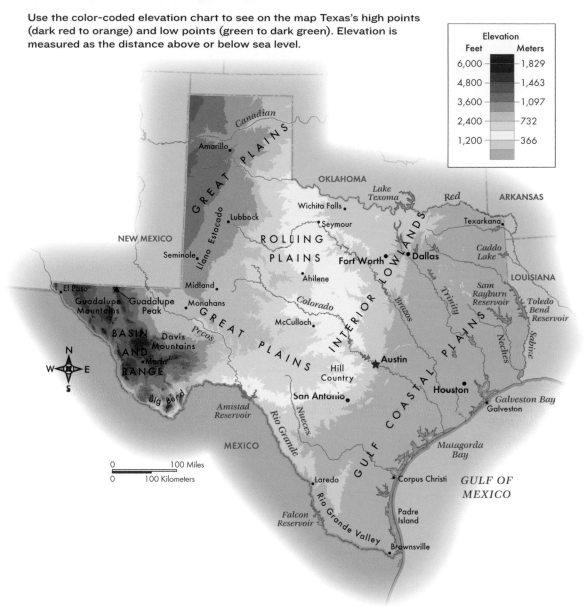

Elevation	
Feet	Meters
6,000	1,829
4,800	1,463
3,600	1,097
2,400	732
1,200	366

ern Texas. As the planet warmed and the ice melted, the runoff water carved rivers deep in the earth. Tall grasses flourished on the plains. Wildlife thrived. Texas evolved into the place we know today.

Rafters on the Rio Grande floating through the Santa Elena Canyon near Big Bend National Park

LAND REGIONS

Texas sits in the southern part of the United States, where the South meets the Southwest. To the east are Louisiana and a tiny corner of Arkansas, while New Mexico lies to the west. To the north is Oklahoma. The square piece of Texas that juts up next to the main part of Oklahoma is called the Texas Panhandle. The Rio Grande separates Texas from the nation of Mexico in the southwest, and in the southeast, the warm waters of the Gulf of Mexico lap against the Texas shoreline.

Texas has four major regions: the Gulf Coastal Plains, the Great Plains, the Interior Lowlands, and the Basin and Range. Each region has its own character, climate, plants, and animals.

Gulf Coastal Plains

The Gulf Coastal Plains lies along Texas's southeastern border. Thin **barrier islands**, including Padre Island, run along the coast. These islands attract seabirds, sea turtles, and tourists. Summers are hot and humid. Besides beaches, this area includes miles of marsh and grasslands, interrupted by clusters of oaks. Farther inland is the Piney Woods, named for its gently rolling pine-covered hills. This area contains two types of wetlands: bayous and sloughs. Bayous are sluggish, swampy bodies of water, while sloughs are small standing pools of water.

WORD TO KNOW

barrier islands *islands that are created by the gradual buildup of sand and stones from the ocean floor*

Texas Geo-Facts

Along with the state's geographical highlights, this chart ranks Texas's land, water, and total area compared to all other states.

Total area; rank . . . . 268,581 square miles (695,625 sq km); 2nd
Land; rank. . . . . 261,797 square miles (678,054 sq km); 2nd
Water; rank . . . . .6,784 square miles (17,571 sq km); 9th
Inland water; rank. . . . . 5,056 square miles (13,095 sq km); 2nd
Coastal water; rank. . . . . 404 square miles (1,046 sq km); 13th
Territorial water; rank . . . . .1,324 square miles (3,429 sq km); 7th
Geographic center . . . . McCulloch, 15 miles (24 km) northeast of Brady
Latitude . . . . .36° to 46° N
Longitude . . . . 94° to 106° W
Highest point. . . . . Guadalupe Peak, 8,749 feet (2,667 m)
Lowest point . . . . .Sea level along the Gulf of Mexico
Largest city . . . . .Houston
Longest river . . . . Rio Grande, 1,240 miles (1,996 km)

Source: U.S. Census Bureau

Add up the areas of Ohio, Indiana, Maine, New Hampshire, Rhode Island, Vermont, Connecticut, New York, New Jersey, Maryland, Delaware, and Pennsylvania— that's the size of Texas (with 1,673 square miles, or 4,333 sq km, left over)!

Great Plains

The Great Plains is a vast grassland that stretches from Canada across the middle of the United States all the way to Texas. In the Texas Panhandle, it is called the High Plains. Here the wind blows nearly all the time. More than 19,000 playa lakes dot the land. These are water holes that fill with rain in the spring and dry up by the fall. The High Plains are on a high, level plateau sometimes called the Llano Estacado, which is Spanish for "palisaded plain." A palisade is a fence made of wooden stakes. The name may refer to the steep mesas that rise around the plain. This dry region is a major producer of cotton and other crops, though, thanks to groundwater pumped from deep beneath the surface.

Prairie dogs dig extensive cities on the High Plains. Their empty burrows attract interesting critters—harm-

A field of cotton is harvested in the High Plains region.

less burrowing owls and not-so-harmless rattlesnakes. In the early 20th century, artist Georgia O'Keeffe spent four years in the Panhandle, where she made paintings of the stark plains that drew national attention. She said of the region, "That was my country—terrible winds and a wonderful emptiness."

In central Texas, the Great Plains become an area of rolling hills and steep valleys called the Hill Country. The capital city of Austin is just beyond the eastern edge of this region. In the Hill Country, mesquite trees pop up among short grasses and cacti. According to Texas lore, nothing can kill a mesquite tree, and many are hundreds of years old.

Interior Lowlands

The land is low and rolling in the Interior Lowlands, which stretch across north-central and northeastern Texas. The area, which is made of three plains regions, is wetter than the Great Plains and supports agriculture and some hardwood forests.

Basin and Range

The Basin and Range is sometimes called the Trans-Pecos region because it consists of the land west of the Pecos River (*trans* means "across"). In the Basin and Range, rugged mountains alternate with broad, flat basins. This is dry country. Annually, the region gets only 12 inches (30 centimeters) of rain. The highest mountain in Texas, Guadalupe Peak, rises in the northern Trans-Pecos. In the southern Trans-Pecos, the Rio Grande makes a large curve, forming a region called the Big Bend. Harsh but beautiful Big Bend National Park features twisting rocky mountains, cool rivers, and vast deserts that support a surprising amount of life.

SEE IT HERE!

MARFA LIGHTS

For more than 100 years, people have seen strange lights dancing in the West Texas sky. The origin of these lights is a mystery. Suggestions about what they are range from ghosts to burning swamp gas to reflections of moonlight off mica. To this day, no one knows. The Marfa lights are seen every clear night about 10 miles (16 km) east of the town of Marfa.

Weather Report

TEMPERATURE 120°F **TEMPERATURE -23°F**

This chart shows record temperatures (high and low) for the state, as well as average temperatures (July and January) and average annual precipitation.

Record high temperature . . . . 120°F (49°C) at Seymour on August 12, 1936, and at Monahans on June 28, 1994

Record low temperature . . . . –23°F (–31°C) at Julia on February 12, 1899, and at Seminole on February 8, 1933

Average July temperature . . . . 85°F (29°C)

Average January temperature . . . . 44°F (7°C)

Average annual precipitation . . . . 34 inches (86 cm)

Source: National Climatic Data Center, NESDIS, NOAA, U.S. Department of Commerce

WORD TO KNOW

precipitation *all water that falls to the earth, including rain, sleet, hail, snow, dew, fog, or mist*

On April 14, 1935, a thick blanket of dust covered miles of Texas, blocking out the sunlight and making the middle of the afternoon as dark as night. The day the storm hit became known as Black Sunday.

CLIMATE

The best description of Texas's climate is "changeable." In central and northern Texas, winters are cold and summers are hot. Both seasons are windy, and there is a moderate amount of **precipitation**. In the Panhandle, winter winds often bring snow flurries or ice storms. The mountains of West Texas are colder. Summers are milder, and rainfall is less common. In fact, parts of the Trans-Pecos are desert. In the southeast, humid air blows in from the Gulf of Mexico. Summers are hot and sticky, and rain is plentiful.

EXTREME WEATHER

Texans have learned to laugh about their weather. They claim to have four seasons: drought, flood, blizzard, and twister.

Drought cycles often last five years or more. Too little rain can cause crops and livestock to die. Dust storms are another disastrous result of drought. Withered grasses can't hold the soil in place. When strong winds blow through, they pick up the soil and carry it along in massive clouds. During droughts, the soil is baked hard, so when it does finally rain, water runs off the soil instead of being absorbed into the ground. This fast-moving runoff creates flash floods.

Hurricanes threaten the Texas coast from July through October. North Texas lies in the southernmost part of "Tornado Alley," a swath of land particularly prone to tornadoes. The state endures an average of 126

tornadoes a year. Not all tornadoes cause tremendous damage, but schools have tornado drills so that students and staff know how to find safety just in case.

RIVERS AND LAKES

Texas is awfully wet for such a dry state. It has 3,700 named streams, 15 major rivers, 212 **reservoirs**, the Panhandle's 19,000-plus playa lakes, and thousands of square miles of swamps, bayous, and other wetlands.

The state's longest river is the Rio Grande, Spanish for "big (or great) river." The Rio Grande rises in the San Juan Mountains of Colorado and then rushes south through New Mexico and along the Texas-Mexico border before emptying into the Gulf of Mexico. During its 1,240-mile (1,996 km) run, it is at times a trickle and at times rushing whitewater rapids. It ends in a wide, sluggish river.

Other major rivers in the state include the Colorado, the Trinity, and the Brazos. Dams form most of Texas's largest lakes, although there are a few natural lakes. One of the largest natural lakes is Caddo Lake, along the Louisiana border. Caddo Lake is filled with channels, inlets, and cypress forests. The area around the lake has 189 species of trees and shrubs, abundant wild grasses, and a host of animals, many of them **endangered**.

WORDS TO KNOW

reservoirs *artificial lakes or tanks created for water storage*

endangered *in danger of becoming extinct*

The trunk of a bald cypress tree rises from Caddo Lake.

PLANT LIFE

Once, 470 species of wild grasses covered the plains of Texas. Today, the endless seas of grass have given way to ranches, wheat and hay farms, housing developments, and roads. Wild grasses—such as fescue grass, buffalo grass, hairy grama, Indian grass, tall dropseed, and sideoats grama—grow from 2 to 13 feet (0.6 to 4 m) tall and send roots deep into the soil.

More than 5,000 varieties of wildflowers paint the remaining grasslands brilliant yellows, vital reds, and sky blues. From bluebonnets—the state flower—to black-foot daisies and black-eyed Susans, Texas meadows shine with color. Some wildflowers have names that tell what they look like: Mexican hat, wine-cups, spider lilies, and pitcher plants.

Texas has more than 100 species of cacti, from baby burro tail to bird's nest to dead man's fingers. Prickly pear cactus flowers come in colors from yellow to deep purple. Ocotillo cactus looks like a spider lying on its back. It sports deep red flowers on its slim branches. The flowers on the Texas rainbow cactus are hot yellows and oranges.

Longleaf, shortleaf, and loblolly pines dominate the Piney Woods. It also has stands of oak, ash, and hickory.

Rainbow cactus in bloom

Texas National Park Areas

This map shows some of Texas's national parks, monuments, preserves, and other areas protected by the National Park Service.

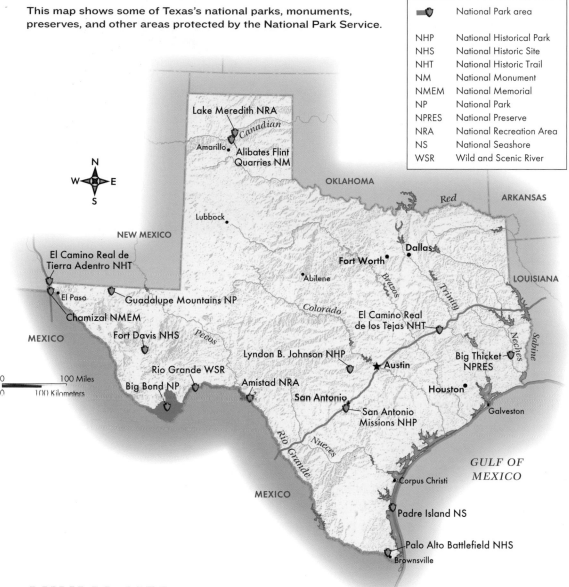

	National Park area
NHP	National Historical Park
NHS	National Historic Site
NHT	National Historic Trail
NM	National Monument
NMEM	National Memorial
NP	National Park
NPRES	National Preserve
NRA	National Recreation Area
NS	National Seashore
WSR	Wild and Scenic River

Lake Meredith NRA
Amarillo
Alibates Flint Quarries NM
OKLAHOMA
Red
ARKANSAS
Lubbock
NEW MEXICO
El Camino Real de Tierra Adentro NHT
El Paso
Guadalupe Mountains NP
Chamizal NMEM
MEXICO
Fort Davis NHS
Pecos
Rio Grande WSR
Big Bend NP
Amistad NRA
San Antonio
San Antonio Missions NHP
Fort Worth
Abilene
Dallas
Brazos
Trinity
LOUISIANA
Colorado
El Camino Real de los Tejas NHT
Lyndon B. Johnson NHP
Austin
Big Thicket NPRES
Neches
Sabine
Houston
Galveston
Rio Grande
Nueces
GULF OF MEXICO
MEXICO
Corpus Christi
Padre Island NS
Palo Alto Battlefield NHS
Brownsville
Canadian

100 Miles
100 Kilometers

ANIMAL LIFE

A wide variety of animals populate Texas, ranging from wolves to prairie dogs, **javelinas** to armadillos, and horned lizards to whooping cranes. Cougars prowl the mountains and deserts, coyotes hunt on the plains, and

WORD TO KNOW

javelinas *wild, piglike creatures with razor-sharp tusks*

Roseate spoonbills wading along the coast near Galveston

ENDANGERED SPECIES

Among the state's many endangered and threatened creatures are peregrine falcons, whales, dolphins, manatees, wolves, bears, black-footed ferrets, coatis, ocelots, margays, and jaguarundis. Coatis are raccoon-like creatures with long tails. Ocelots, and their smaller cousins margays, look like small leopards. Jaguarundis resemble small mountain lions.

Black-footed ferret

black bear feed on wild berries in the woods. White-tailed deer, which number about 2.5 million, live just about everywhere. The state's 200,000 alligators keep to the swamps and bayous. Along the coast, roseate spoonbills wade through the marsh reeds in search of food. Texas has more than 100 species of snakes; most are harmless. The dangerous ones include rattlesnakes, cottonmouths, and coral snakes. Although many people are afraid of snakes, they are actually helpful to humans because they eat lizards, mice, and rats that would otherwise damage crops.

PROTECTING WILDLIFE

As humans have turned grasslands into ranches, and wetlands into housing developments, many animals in Texas have become endangered. In 1941, only 15 whooping cranes survived worldwide. Many people went to work to try to preserve the whooping crane's habitat so that they could survive. Now Aransas National Wildlife Refuge along the Gulf Coast is home to the nation's largest population of whooping cranes. Each spring, more than 200 whooping cranes spread their wings and head to Canada to their summer nesting grounds. In the fall, they return to the refuge, hopefully bringing dozens of young birds with them.

Padre Island National Seashore protects a group of barrier islands where the most endangered sea turtle in the world—the Kemp's ridley sea turtle—nests. The park participates in a program to ensure the survival of these rare sea turtles. Volunteers monitor the beaches to safeguard the nests where the precious eggs are buried.

MINI-BIO

RALPH WEBSTER YARBOROUGH: TEXAS ENVIRONMENTALIST

Born in Chandler, Ralph Webster Yarborough (1903–1996) served in the armed forces during World War II. After the war, he became a lawyer and eventually a U.S. senator. He wrote laws to establish Padre Island National Seashore and Guadalupe Mountains National Park. He cowrote the Endangered Species Act and sponsored a law to protect the golden eagle. Because of Yarborough's efforts, animals in Texas have a better chance of survival.

? Want to know more? See www.tshaonline.org/handbooks/online/articles/YY/fyags.html

Naturalists Linda McGonigle (left) and Dita Strohmeyer gather information about Kemp's ridley sea turtles at Padre Island.

READ ABOUT

Native Americans
hunted buffalo
for food, clothing,
and shelter.

c. 9000 BCE
*Humans arrive in
what is now Texas*

c. 3000 BCE
*The Statean culture
is at its height*

▲ c. 2500 BCE
*People begin
growing crops*

CHAPTER TWO

FIRST PEOPLE

★

DESERTS AND SWAMPS, DROUGHTS AND FLOODS, TORNADOES AND HURRICANES—ALL THESE CONDITIONS CAN MAKE LIVING IN TEXAS DIFFICULT TODAY. Yet humans arrived in Texas more than 11,000 years ago and managed to thrive. Living in groups, they moved about, hunting mammoths, buffalo, and other huge beasts and gathering edible plants.

c. 2500–1000 BCE

People settle in villages

700 CE ▶

People begin using pottery for storage and cooking

800

Mound Builders begin creating large ceremonial mounds

SEE IT HERE!

ROCK ART

Scientists believe the Jumano people drew some of the oldest examples of rock art in North America in the Fate Bell area of Seminole Canyon State Park. These pictographs show group life, animals, and hunting. Many of the drawings are life-size, and experts have identified several different styles of art.

WORD TO KNOW

pictographs *pictures drawn on rocks or cave walls*

These pictographs were created thousands of years ago in what is now Seminole Canyon State Historical Park.

EARLY HUNTER-GATHERERS

These early people are called hunter-gatherers because they survived by hunting and gathering food found in the wild. Their primary tool for hunting was a spear, and the hunters worked in groups to kill and butcher animals. While men hunted, women and children collected nuts, berries, fruits, and roots. Early people who lived near the sea also ate clams, mussels, and fish. Wherever they went, they looked for shelter in caves. They cooked on open fires and turned animal hides into clothes.

SETTLING DOWN

In time, people began recording the stories of their lives on rocks. By at least 3000 BCE, people in what is now West Texas began making pictures on the rocks along the lower Pecos River. They used several different colors to make **pictographs** depicting humans and animals.

Between 2500 and 1000 BCE, people began growing crops. The first crops were most likely squash, beans, and corn. Farming provided a steady supply of food,

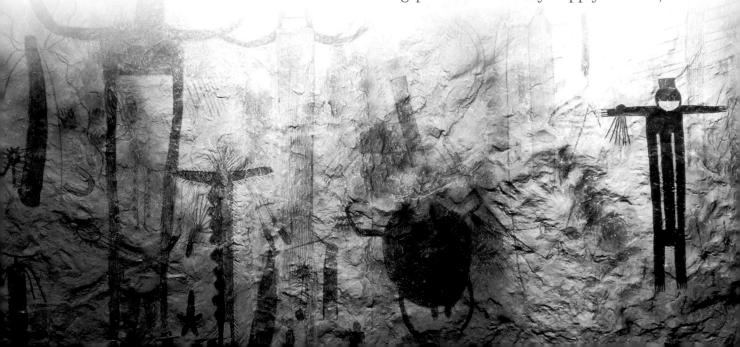

This pathway leads to the Caddoan Mounds, which still stand in Alto today.

so people could stay in one place. They began making villages and creating cemeteries for their dead. By 700 CE, the Native people had begun hunting with bows and arrows. These were more effective than spears. By this time, people had also developed pottery for cooking and food storage.

MOUND BUILDERS

By 800, some villagers were building large earth mounds. Some mounds appear to have been cemeteries. Others may have been used for religious purposes. **Archaeologists** are still trying to determine what the mounds were really for. They have discovered **obsidian** tools and ceremonial objects in some mounds. But obsidian doesn't come from Texas. This gave scientists an interesting puzzle to solve. Where did the obsidian come from? They tested its chemistry and found that it matched samples from today's Idaho, Wyoming, and northern Mexico. This showed that people in Texas had already established trade with people in other regions.

WORDS TO KNOW

archaeologists *people who study the remains of past human societies*

obsidian *jet-black volcanic glass*

Native American Peoples
(Before European Contact)

This map shows the general area of Native American peoples before
European settlers arrived.

NATIVE AMERICAN CULTURES

Over time, the villages grew into groups and distinct cultures. Various peoples lived along the Gulf of Mexico. Using branches and animal hides, they built shelters that could be taken apart quickly and moved to another area. The Caddo people, who are also called the Hasinai, lived in the Piney Woods of East Texas. They used stone axes to cut down trees. The trees became the framework for their large, cone-shaped houses. Caddos covered the log framework with long grasses.

The Jumano people lived in the Big Bend region. Some lived in houses cut into cliff walls. Others built shelters using adobe bricks made of sun-dried earth.

By 1500, all of the groups had thrived for centuries. But for many of them, change was just around the corner. Strangers from Spain would soon arrive.

A Native American settlement near the Gulf of Mexico

READ ABOUT

A Spanish conquistador, wearing armor and on horseback, explores the region that became Texas.

1528 ▲

Álvar Núñez Cabeza de Vaca is shipwrecked in Texas

1540–1542

Francisco Vásquez de Coronado leads an expedition into Texas

1682

The first Texas mission is founded

EXPLORATION AND SETTLEMENT

CHAPTER THREE

EXPLORATION AND SETTLEMENT

★

IN THE 1500s, A NEW GROUP OF PEOPLE ARRIVED IN TEXAS. Spanish explorers came from Europe, across the Atlantic Ocean. They wanted three things from North America: a quick route to China, wealth, and power. The shortcut to China did not exist, and wealth was scarce. So the Spanish conquerors, called conquistadores, settled for power. As part of that power, they tried to spread their religion, Roman Catholicism, throughout the land.

◄1822
Stephen F. Austin establishes Texas's first Anglo-American colony

1835
The Texas Revolution begins

1836
Texas wins its independence

CONQUISTADORES FROM SPAIN

When the Spaniards conquered the Aztec empire in Mexico in 1521, they captured a treasure in gold, silver, and gems. From that point on, Spanish explorers in North America set off on treasure hunts. The Spanish conquistadores did not hesitate to kill or torture Native people in their quest for riches.

The first Europeans known to set foot in Texas were a group of Spaniards led by Álvar Núñez Cabeza de Vaca who landed on the Florida coast in 1528. With no supplies or horses, the men wandered through the wilderness. By 1532, only four men remained. One of them, Estévanico, was an enslaved man from Morocco, a region of North Africa. Estévanico quickly mastered Indian languages and broke through cultural barriers. Cabeza de Vaca reported that he "was our go-between; he informed himself about the ways we wished to take, what towns there were, and the matters we desired to know." Talking with various peoples, Estévanico heard many tales of legendary cities filled with gold. The four lost men slowly found their way through the hot, dry, harsh land to Mexico City, the capital of New Spain, the Spanish colony in North America. They had been lost for eight years.

In 1539, Spanish officials chose Estévanico as the advance scout for a group that would explore the Southwest searching for the

MINI-BIO

ÁLVAR NÚÑEZ CABEZA DE VACA: FIRST SPANIARD IN TEXAS

Álvar Núñez Cabeza de Vaca (1490?–1557?) was a well-educated Spaniard who joined the military as a young man. He led what proved to be a disastrous eight-year journey through Florida, Texas, and Mexico. Cabeza de Vaca (seen here on a Spanish postage stamp) later wrote of his travels, giving Europeans their first view of Native groups in Texas. He eventually returned to Spain, where he served as a judge until his death.

? Want to know more? See www.pbs.org/weta/thewest/people/a_c/cabezadevaca.htm

European Exploration of Texas

The colored arrows on this map show the routes taken by European explorers between 1519 and 1687.

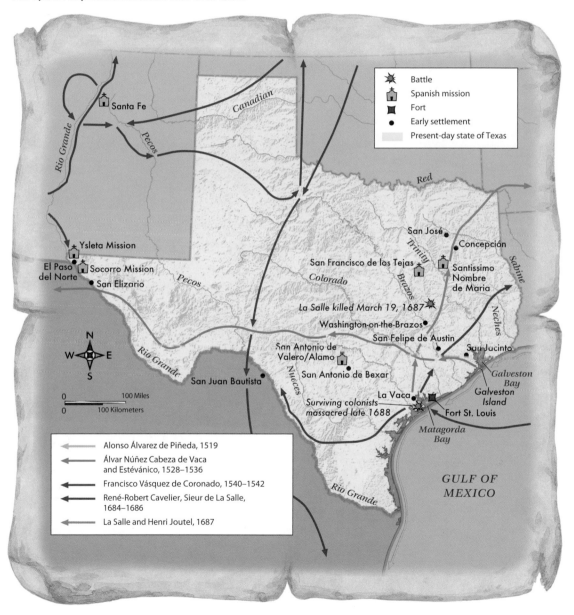

Legend:
- Battle
- Spanish mission
- Fort
- Early settlement
- Present-day state of Texas

Santa Fe

Canadian

Rio Grande

Pecos

Ysleta Mission

El Paso del Norte

Socorro Mission

San Elizario

Pecos

Red

San José

Trinity

Concepción

San Francisco de los Tejas

Colorado

Brazos

Santissimo Nombre de Maria

Sabine

La Salle killed March 19, 1687

Washington-on-the-Brazos

Neches

San Felipe de Austin

San Antonio de Valero/Alamo

San Jacinto

Río Grande

San Juan Bautista

Nueces

San Antonio de Bexar

La Vaca

Galveston Bay

Galveston Island

Surviving colonists massacred late 1688

Fort St. Louis

Matagorda Bay

GULF OF MEXICO

N W E S

Río Grande

0   100 Miles
0   100 Kilometers

Alonso Álvarez de Piñeda, 1519

Álvar Núñez Cabeza de Vaca and Estévánico, 1528–1536

Francisco Vásquez de Coronado, 1540–1542

René-Robert Cavelier, Sieur de La Salle, 1684–1686

La Salle and Henri Joutel, 1687

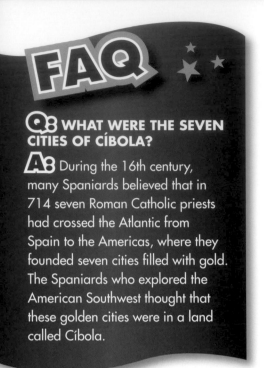

FAQ

Q8 WHAT WERE THE SEVEN CITIES OF CÍBOLA?

A8 During the 16th century, many Spaniards believed that in 714 seven Roman Catholic priests had crossed the Atlantic from Spain to the Americas, where they founded seven cities filled with gold. The Spaniards who explored the American Southwest thought that these golden cities were in a land called Cíbola.

WORD TO KNOW

expedition *a trip for the purpose of exploration*

mythical Seven Cities of Cíbola, cities made of gold. The Spaniards found no golden cities, but they continued to search. From 1540 to 1542, Francisco Vásquez de Coronado led an **expedition** onto the Llano Estacado—the plains of the Texas Panhandle. They found a high plateau cut by deep canyons, a sea of dense grass, and many Native villages, but no gold.

Around the same time, another Spanish expedition moved westward from Florida. In 1542, they entered Texas from the east and became the first Spaniards to contact the Hasinai (Caddo) people. The Caddos welcomed the newcomers. But contact with the Europeans proved to be a disaster for the Caddos. They died of common European diseases such as measles and smallpox, to which they had never before been exposed. Disease wiped out entire villages, and the Caddos grew to distrust the outsiders.

Francisco Vásquez de Coronado setting out on his expedition in 1540

The Spanish lost interest in Texas when they realized there was no gold to be found. No more Spaniards arrived until a dozen years later, when three Spanish ships sank near Padre Island. The ships carried a fortune in silver and gold. Finally, there were riches in Texas—lying under deep water in the Gulf of Mexico.

NATIVE AMERICANS MIGRATE

Native Americans continued to arrive in Texas after the Spanish explored the region. They included the Lipan Apaches, the Comanches, and the Wichitas.

Lipan Apaches

The Lipan Apaches, or Tindis—"Warriors of the Mountains"—spread from New Mexico eastward into the Panhandle and south-central Texas. The Lipans moved from place to place, hunting for food. They stayed in a region long enough to plant, raise, and harvest crops or hunt the available game. Then they moved on. Women planted crops of corn, beans, squash, and melons to feed their group through long, cold winters. When a couple got married, the husband moved in with his wife's family. If a wife died, her family supplied a new bride for the widower. The Lipans were skilled warriors. They forced the Caddos to move to the south and east. By the early 1700s, the Lipans settled along the Rio Grande.

The Spanish had introduced horses to Texas, and the Lipan Apaches became excellent horseback riders. They attacked and raided settlements for food and more horses. Despite their superb fighting skills, they were no match for the Comanches and the Wichitas, who had traded with the French for European weapons. Bows and arrows could not compete with guns.

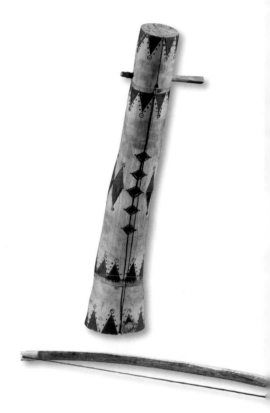

This Apache musical instrument, called a *tsii'edo'a'tl*, is played like a violin.

The Wichitas

The Wichitas ranged through today's Kansas, Oklahoma, and as far south as the Brazos River of Texas. They set up permanent villages and depended on agriculture and bison hunting for food. In good years, the villages produced extra corn or squash, which they traded with neighboring groups.

Each Wichita village featured a cone-shaped building that served as a community center, sleeping room, cook station, and meeting place. These buildings were about 30 to 50 feet (9 to 15 m) across. They were made of strong wooden poles covered with thatch. In the center, a fireplace was used for heating and cooking. A hole in the roof directly above the fire pit allowed smoke to escape. People slept on raised platforms around the edge of the building.

The Wichitas called themselves *kitikitish*, or "raccoon eyes." This name comes from the lines that Wichita men tattooed on their eyelids. The women tattooed lines on their chins. Complex tattoos also decorated the chests of older community members.

Comanches

Comanches emerged as a group on the northern plains and in the Rocky Mountains. They migrated southward in the 1700s. They called themselves Numunuh—"the people." The name Comanche came later from a rival group's word for "enemy."

Comanches were organized into communities, each with a peace chief and a council. Usually, the peace chief was a wise, older

DEATH OF A COMANCHE WARRIOR

Elderly retired warriors often gathered at the Smoke Lodge. There they recalled past victories and waited to die. When a man died, the women bathed his body and painted his face red. The body was folded up with the knees close to the chest and the arms down by the sides. The body was tied with rope and placed on a horse or pony. A woman mounted the horse behind the body and rode to the final burial place.

The warrior was buried in a cave or in a deep crack in the rocks. His weapons were broken and laid by his side. His saddle was placed with the body. Many times, the warrior's best pony was taken to the burial site and killed. For a chief, many ponies would be killed. This honored the dead because ponies were wealth. Comanches used ponies for gifts, trade, and war. The sacrifice of a pony was a great honor.

person whose opinion was respected. The council also consisted of older, experienced men. If the council decided to go to war, it chose a war chief, who functioned like a general. All warriors had to follow the war chief's orders.

Comanches were fierce fighters. As they expanded their territory on the Great Plains, they pushed out tribes that lived on those lands. Like Lipan Apaches, they raided their enemies, sometimes obtaining horses in the process. Comanches were also known to attack wagons that were carrying settlers heading West.

Comanches cherished children, and rarely punished them. All children learned to ride horses as toddlers and could handle horses with skill by age five or six. Boys received their first bows and arrows at about six years old. Although girls and women could ride, they generally were not involved in hunting. Girls were close to their mothers and aunts, who taught them how to cook, sew, and store food. Women were highly respected in Comanche culture and were considered valued members of the group.

A Comanche warrior

Spanish missionaries and Native Americans after a religious ceremony at the Alamo mission

FOUNDING MISSIONS

Spain did not return its attention to Texas until the late 1600s. Rather than establish Spanish cities in Texas, the plan was to turn Native Americans into loyal, taxpaying Spaniards. Ignoring Native beliefs, Spain sent Roman Catholic priests to New Spain to establish **missions** and convert the Native Americans to Catholicism. The Spanish wanted the Indians to wear European clothes, speak Spanish, and develop European habits.

Besides converting the Native peoples to Catholicism, the Spanish had another motivation for establishing missions in Texas. Spain was not the only nation that had interests in claims to Texas lands. Though Spaniards were the first Europeans to explore the Texas region, France's René-Robert Cavelier, Sieur de La Salle, claimed the region for his country in 1682. The Spanish were worried they would lose their lands in Texas to France, or other nations for that matter.

The Spaniards founded the first mission in Texas at Corpus Christi de la Ysleta, near present-day El Paso,

in 1682. This early mission did not succeed. In 1690, the Spanish founded a second mission near villages of the Hasinai. The mission lasted about three years. Many Hasinai died from European diseases, and the Hasinai began avoiding the priests. Meanwhile, floods destroyed the mission gardens. Indian raids frightened the priests. They closed the mission and headed back to the safety of Mexico City.

Almost 30 years later, the Spanish tried to establish yet another set of missions, this time across central Texas. One of these, San Antonio de Valero Mission, is better known as the Alamo. The San Antonio mission was a success, primarily because it served as a trading post as well as a mission. Between 1718 and 1731, nearly 50 couples married in the mission chapel, and more than 100 children were baptized there. San Antonio served as a supply station between one mission and the next, and it became the most profitable community in Spanish Texas. To Spain, the San Antonio mission was a huge success.

Many Native Americans had a different view. Thousands died from European diseases. Spanish soldiers enslaved them to work in the fields. And most Indians had no desire to give up their traditions or religious beliefs. They resented the priests and the military, and often attacked mission property. The Comanches and Apaches raided livestock herds, killed soldiers, and burned settlers' homes. Native attacks forced many Spanish missions to close. But the newcomers never gave up any of the land they took.

SEE IT HERE!

EL PASO MISSIONS

Take a step into history by visiting the missions near El Paso. The missions of Ysleta del Sur and Socorro and the San Elizario Chapel show the influence of the Indians who helped build them. The Ysleta del Sur Pueblo Cultural Center includes a museum of the Tigua people, the Native Americans of the area. At the cultural center, visitors can learn about Tigua art and taste Tigua foods.

The mission of Ysleta del Sur as it appears today

MEXICAN INDEPENDENCE

Mexicans had long resented Spanish control over Mexico. It seemed to many that Spain took much of Mexico's wealth, while providing little in return. The 13 British colonies had recently rebelled to become the United States of America. Mexico, too, wanted its independence.

In 1810, Father Miguel Hidalgo y Costilla urged Mexicans to rebel, starting a fight for independence. After rebels captured Zacatecas, San Luis Potosí, and Valladolid, Hidalgo organized a march on Mexico City.

In the Mexican province of Texas, José Bernardo Gutiérrez de Lara and Augustus W. Magee formed a rebel band in 1812. They planned to capture land in Texas with the hope of eventually creating an independent state. They recruited soldiers by offering $40 per month and Texas land. The Texas rebels captured Nacogdoches, La Bahia, and San Antonio but were ultimately crushed by the Spanish forces.

Spain also faced unrest in other colonies. Rebellions in Chile, Peru, Argentina, and Venczuela stretched Spain's military resources thin.

Mexico finally won its freedom from Spanish rule in 1821. The war had lasted 11 years and drained the new country's resources. Thousands of men could not find work. Mexico needed strong leaders to solve the economic problems left in the wake of war. Unfortunately, the country's new leaders had little government experience. They tried to turn the economy around by opening Mexican land to settlers, including English or white settlers, known as Anglos.

Father Miguel Hidalgo y Costilla

ANGLOS ARRIVE

The government offered grants to wealthy men to establish colonies on Mexican land. The grant holders were called *empresarios*. One of the first *empresarios* was Stephen F. Austin, who was originally from Virginia. The founding of Anglo-American settlements in Texas encouraged more settlers to move there from the United States. When Mexico became independent, about 2,500 Spaniards, Mexicans, African Americans, and Anglos lived in Texas. But as cities opened up and ranches expanded, there was much work to be done and money to be earned. American settlers poured into Texas, bring-

MINI-BIO

STEPHEN FULLER AUSTIN: THE FATHER OF TEXAS

Stephen Fuller Austin (1793–1836) was an empresario who was granted land by the Mexican government to establish a colony in Texas. Between 1821 and 1829, Austin encouraged 1,200 families to move into Mexican Texas. In 1835, he urged fellow Texans to revolt against Antonio López de Santa Anna, the self-declared ruler of Mexico. Austin lived to see victory in the Texas revolution and became secretary of state of the Republic of Texas. He died shortly after Texas achieved its independence. Because he established the first successful Anglo-American colony in Texas, he is considered the Father of Texas.

? Want to know more? See www.pbs.org/weta/thewest/people/a_c/austin.htm

Picture Yourself . . .

as a Pioneer Woman
You and your husband have purchased land in that foreign place called Texas. When you arrive on your land, a few hours by wagon from the town called Austin, there is much to be done. You learn how to snare and skin a rabbit and then turn it into a stew. You rise before dawn. You haul water from the creek and fry up bacon and cornmeal cakes for breakfast. You feed the chickens, mules, and horses, and you milk the cow. In the afternoon, you churn cream into butter and bake fresh bread. Harvesttime is coming, and your days will be filled with cutting and threshing wheat and cutting and drying corn. You will also slaughter a pig for bacon, ham, and sausage that you will eat through the winter months. You work 14 hours a day, but it is worth it. You are making a home for your family.

A white overseer watches a group of enslaved workers picking cotton in Texas.

WORD TO KNOW

plantations *large farms that grow mainly one crop*

ing their ideas of economy and government with them. The Anglos of Texas soon outnumbered the Hispanic population.

Although Mexico was still debating the slavery issue, Texas was exempt. Anglo settlers in Texas were slaveholders, and slavery soon became entrenched in Texas. Slavery was as harsh in Texas as it was in the Southern states. Enslaved people worked long, grueling hours, and their families were often separated and sold at auction. Under the watchful eyes of overseers, thousands of slaves picked cotton on **plantations** in East Texas.

Adeline Marshall was enslaved as a child in the Houston area. "You went out to the field almost as soon as you could walk," she later recalled. Cotton sacks were made shorter so children could use them in the fields. Some young men became cowhands. Women and children often served in the plantation house as cooks, seamstresses, and caretakers for children. Other enslaved men and women provided the skills needed to run the plantations, and some became overseers or kept plantation records.

Some Texans—Anglo and Hispanic—resented how the Mexican government ran Texas. Protecting slavery was one concern for Texas. But what greatly alarmed Texans was the Law of April 6, 1830, which, among other things, halted the flow of immigration from the United States into Texas. Santa Anna had also done away with the Constitution of 1824, thereby eliminating elected government. Tensions mounted, and in 1832 and 1835, small rebellions erupted in Texas. Revolution was once more in the air.

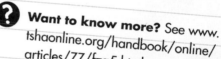

LORENZO DE ZAVALA: A LOVER OF DEMOCRACY

Lorenzo de Zavala (1788–1836) was born on the Yucatán peninsula of Mexico. He served as governor of the state of Mexico, Mexican ambassador to Paris, and the first vice president of the Republic of Texas. He became close friends with Stephen F. Austin, and both men held land grants for settlements in Texas. Zavala was a strong supporter of the Texas independence movement.

? **Want to know more?** See www.tshaonline.org/handbook/online/articles/ZZ/fza5.html

THE TEXAS REVOLUTION

In 1833, Antonio López de Santa Anna became president of Mexico. Two years later, Texan forces seized San Antonio. Both Texans and Mexicans feared that the only way to solve their differences would be war.

The Mexican government had loaned a cannon to the town of Gonzales in what is now south-central Texas. The Mexicans wanted the cannon back, but the Texans refused. On October 2, 1835, an army of 100 Mexicans arrived to retrieve the cannon by force. Instead, they received a barrage of **shrapnel**. The battle for Texan independence had begun.

The Texans chose Sam Houston to be general of their army. Volunteers swelled the ranks of the Texas

WORD TO KNOW

shrapnel *bomb, mine, or shell fragments*

Mexican leader Antonio
López de Santa Anna

army, but the Mexican army was much larger.

In early 1836, Santa Anna led approximately 4,000 Mexican troops to San Antonio. The Texans gathered in the Alamo mission, and Santa Anna's forces surrounded it. William Travis, the leader of the 184 troops inside, scribbled a note to his fellow Texans: "The enemy is receiving reinforcements daily & will no doubt increase to three or four thousand in four or five days. . . . I am determined to sustain myself as long as possible & die like a soldier who never forgets what is due to his own honor & that of his country—Victory or Death."

Santa Anna demanded that the Texans surrender. Instead, they held out for 13 days. Santa Anna's troops then made a final assault on the Alamo. All the Texans in the Alamo died. These men—Jim Bowie, Davy Crockett, William Travis—became the heroes of the Texas Revolution. For generations afterward, Texans spoke proudly of their stubborn bravery. At the time, a Mexican army officer wrote, "Travis was seen to hesitate, but not about the death he would choose. He would take a few steps and stop, turning his proud face toward us to discharge his shots; he fought like a true soldier. Finally he died, but he died after having traded his life very dearly. None of his men died with greater heroism, and they all died. Travis behaved as a hero."

Santa Anna's victory at the Alamo came at a high price. Six hundred Mexican soldiers died or were wounded in the battle. And while the Mexicans had surrounded the Alamo, Sam Houston gathered his troops for a stand at San Jacinto.

On April 21, Houston's army was ready to meet Santa

Anna's army. At about 3:30 in the afternoon, the Mexican soldiers settled down for a rest. Houston placed cannons on either side of the men, and then the Texans stormed forth, shouting, "Remember the Alamo!" The Battle of San Jacinto, such as it was, lasted only 20 minutes. More than 600 Mexican soldiers died and 730 were taken prisoner, including Santa Anna. The Texans lost only nine men. Thus, the revolution ended, and Texas was ready for the next step: forming an independent nation.

This engraving depicts the siege of the Alamo on March 6, 1836.

44

The reading of the constitution at the Texas Constitutional Convention in 1836

1836
The Republic of Texas is formed

▲1845
Texas becomes a state

1846
The first clash of the Mexican-American War takes place in Texas

CHAPTER FOUR

GROWTH AND CHANGE

★

THE DOCUMENT DECLARING THE INDEPENDENCE OF TEXAS HAD BEEN SIGNED. The battles were over. Now came the work of setting up a new nation— the Republic of Texas. Who would run Texas? How would leaders be chosen? Who would be considered citizens, and what rights would they have? Texas needed a constitution.

1861

Texas joins the Confederacy

1867

U.S. troops arrive in Texas to protect the civil rights of people of color

1867–1884 ▶

Cowhands move cattle along the Chisholm Trail

THE REPUBLIC OF TEXAS

On March 1, 1836, 41 representatives from around Texas met in the town of Washington-on-the-Brazos. The members of Texas's constitutional convention chose David Thomas to draft the document, which called for a president, a two-part legislature, and courts that would provide for trial by jury. The new constitution allowed slavery but forbade the international slave trade.

Texans elected Sam Houston president in a landslide, and the Texas Congress met for the first time in Columbia on October 3, 1836. The republic soon enacted a series of laws ensuring that masters maintained control of enslaved people. Laws mandated long prison sentences and heavy fines for anyone who harbored runaway slaves. Meanwhile, more slaveholders moved to Texas from the United States. Free people of color battled hard to keep their rights in Texas.

Protecting Texas's border was another government priority. Texas set the southern border along the Rio Grande, but Mexico disagreed. Mexico insisted the border was farther north, and Mexicans sometimes raided territory claimed by Texas. The new Texas government sent troops to the Rio Grande, increasing tensions.

In addition, relations with Native American groups worsened. Houston hoped to keep the army out of Indian country. African American William Goyens served as Sam Houston's interpreter and diplomat with Native American nations. "We believe him to be a man that will not tell a lie either for the White man or the Red man," said Houston. But negotiations were not always successful. White settlers took Apache, Comanche, and Wichita land for their ranches and farms, forcing Native Americans to leave Texas or fight.

A FIGHT TO STAY FREE

The Ashworths, a family of free blacks, arrived in the early days of the Texas Republic. They became wealthy ranchers and landowners and purchased the liberty of enslaved relatives, hiring them as free laborers. Aaron Ashworth owned 2,570 cattle, and his wife, Mary, owned land valued at $11,000. The Ashworths' wealth and friendship with influential whites helped them defy the republic's discriminatory laws. When a white mob attacked them, the Ashworths organized 150 men, including whites and Hispanics, to fight off the attackers.

Houston formed a corps of rangers with the task of keeping the frontier safe from Indian attacks and controlling the Mexican population. The treaty that ended the war had promised Mexicans their rights, but under the Texas legal system, many Mexican Texan landowners lost vast amounts of property. Mexican Texans saw Houston's rangers as a **bigoted** armed force and a danger to their community. The rangers and the Mexican Texans clashed frequently after Texas became a state.

Sam Houston expanded the Texas Rangers as a way to control the frontier.

WORD TO KNOW

bigoted *having unfair opinions of a group, based on that group's religion, race, or other factors*

MINI-BIO

JUAN CORTINA: A MEXICAN ROBIN HOOD

After witnessing an Anglo marshal abuse a Mexican, Juan Cortina (1824-1894) took up the cause of defending the rights of Mexican Texans. He became a bandit of sorts, and captured the town of Brownsville, Texas, in 1859. Later, he released imprisoned Mexicans whom he felt were being held unjustly. Though Cortina's outlaws struck at white Texans, undermined law and order, and sometimes victimized fellow Mexicans, Mexicans in Texas often saw him as a hero in the mold of Robin Hood. In the 1860s, he became a general of the Mexican Army of the North. In the mid-1870s, American diplomatic pressure led to Cortina's arrest and exile to Mexico City.

? Want to know more? See www.tshaonline.org/handbook/online/articles/CC/fco73.html

Texas: From Territory to Statehood

This map shows the original Texas territory and the area (outlined in red) that became the state of Texas in 1845.

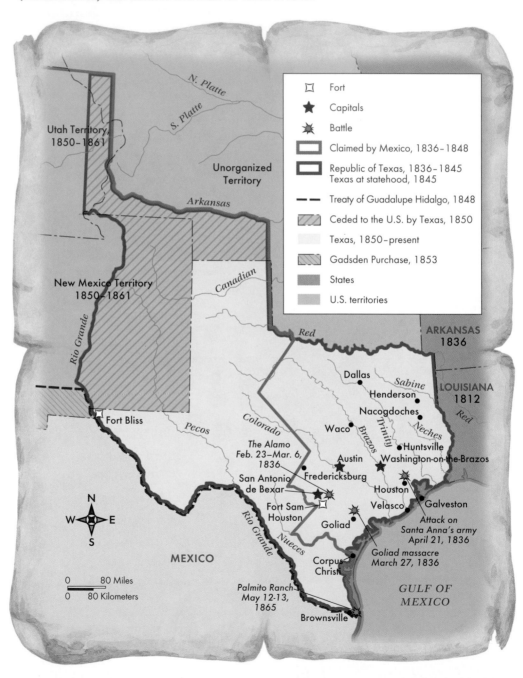

Legend:
- ⬚ Fort
- ★ Capitals
- ✸ Battle
- ▭ Claimed by Mexico, 1836–1848
- ▭ Republic of Texas, 1836–1845 Texas at statehood, 1845
- – – Treaty of Guadalupe Hidalgo, 1848
- ▨ Ceded to the U.S. by Texas, 1850
- ☐ Texas, 1850–present
- ▨ Gadsden Purchase, 1853
- ▨ States
- ☐ U.S. territories

Utah Territory, 1850–1861

Unorganized Territory

N. Platte

S. Platte

Arkansas

New Mexico Territory 1850–1861

Canadian

Rio Grande

Red

ARKANSAS 1836

Dallas

Sabine

Henderson

LOUISIANA 1812

Nacogdoches

Red

Fort Bliss

Pecos

Colorado

Waco

Brazos

Trinity

Neches

Huntsville

The Alamo Feb. 23–Mar. 6, 1836

Austin

Washington-on-the-Brazos

San Antonio de Bexar

Fredericksburg

Houston

Fort Sam Houston

Velasco

Galveston

Goliad

Attack on Santa Anna's army April 21, 1836

Rio Grande

Nueces

Corpus Christi

Goliad massacre March 27, 1836

MEXICO

N W E S

0   80 Miles

0   80 Kilometers

Palmito Ranch May 12-13, 1865

Brownsville

GULF OF MEXICO

This painting depicts the ceremony in which Texas was annexed to the Union.

THE MEXICAN-AMERICAN WAR

Not long after declaring independence, Texas began preparing to join the United States. To become a state, Texas had to write another constitution, and the U.S. Congress had to approve adding Texas to the Union. On December 29, 1845, President James K. Polk signed the document **annexing** Texas as a state.

The United States and Mexico were soon heading toward war. The two countries disagreed about the border. The United States also wanted to purchase California and New Mexico. The Mexican government was still furious over losing Texas and opposed American interest in California. Polk ordered troops to the Texas-Mexico border, and on April 25, 1846, the Mexican army clashed with the U.S. Army. Mexico was determined to take back Texas; the United States was determined to defeat Mexico.

WORD TO KNOW

annexing *uniting; incorporating territory into a country*

The Battle of Palo Alto, on May 8, 1846, was one conflict in the Mexican-American War.

Many Northerners in the United States opposed the war. Congressman Abraham Lincoln charged that President Polk started the war to gain new territory. Others believed it was a plot by slaveholders to acquire new land for slave states, which would add proslavery senators and representatives to a U.S. Congress that was divided over the issue.

After nearly two years of battles, the two countries signed the Treaty of Guadalupe Hidalgo in February 1848. The treaty set Texas's southern border at the Rio Grande. The United States also gained California, Arizona, New Mexico, and parts of Colorado, Nevada, and Utah. Mexico lost half of its territory. The United States paid $15 million for the land.

THE ANTISLAVERY MOVEMENT

After Texas entered the Union, resistance by enslaved people increased and violence escalated. Enslaved men and women in Texas found white allies. Unlike other

Southern states, Texas did not ban educating enslaved people, and by 1860, an estimated 8,000 enslaved Texans had learned to read. The wives of white planters had taught many of them. German immigrants were at the forefront of the antislavery movement in Texas. They held a large antislavery protest meeting in Galveston in 1854. Others helped runaways reach safety in Mexico.

TEXAS JOINS THE CONFEDERACY

By 1860, the long debate over slavery between Northern and Southern states was about to burst into violence. The following year, 11 Southern slaveholding states left the Union and formed the Confederate States of America, or the Confederacy. Although Texas joined them, Governor Sam Houston refused to support the Confederacy. "I love Texas too well to bring civil strife and bloodshed upon her," he proclaimed. For his support of the Union, Confederates drove Houston from public office.

Over the course of the Civil War, 90,000 Texans served in the Confederate army, mostly in the **cavalry**. In 1860, the population of Texas was 604,215, and nearly 183,000 of the total were enslaved workers, so the percentage of Texans serving in the military was high. More than 2,000 white and Mexican Texans and 47 black Texans joined the Union army. During the war, many people fleeing slavery sought safety in

MINI-BIO

SAM HOUSTON: PATRIOT

Sam Houston (1793–1863) was born on a Virginia plantation. He became a lawyer and a congressman from Tennessee. He was living in Texas at the time of the Texas Revolution, and he became the leader of the Texas army. He served as president of the Republic of Texas and, after Texas became a state, as governor. Houston also served as U.S. senator for 13 years. Although he was a slaveholder, he refused to support Texas leaving the Union, a stance that negatively affected his career in public service.

? Want to know more? See www.tshaonline. org/handbook/online/articles/HH/fho73.html

WORD TO KNOW

cavalry *soldiers who ride on horseback*

Bales of cotton piled up at Brownsville while Union forces occupied the city during the Civil War.

Picture Yourself ...

at a Juneteenth Celebration

Today is June 19, 1865. The Civil War ended more than two months ago, but as of yesterday, you were still enslaved and yearning for freedom. There weren't enough Union troops in Texas to enforce President Lincoln's order freeing the enslaved people. But today, General Gordon Granger has finally landed at Galveston to officially announce the end of slavery. The news triggers celebrations throughout the city. You join other formerly enslaved people in a parade, singing and shouting to the beat of joyful drums. Full of hope for the future, you fall asleep that night making plans for a reunion with the family you've been separated from for years. More than a century later, your descendants will still celebrate Juneteenth every June 19.

Mexico, and white Texans helped them. Meanwhile, as Union forces invaded the Southeast, slaveholders from other states drove 150,000 enslaved men, women, and children to Texas to keep them from being freed.

Because Texas was so far west, few Civil War battles took place there. Still, ordinary Texans suffered during the war. The Union army blocked Texas ports, and household products became scarce. The final battle of the Civil War occurred at Palmito Ranch near Brownsville, Texas, on May 13, 1865, a month after the Confederate army had surrendered in Virginia.

RECONSTRUCTION

By the war's end, the Texas government had no money, the capitol in Austin had no roof, and disorder reigned. A newspaper described a state filled with "ruffians and lawless men." Texas became the most violent state in the years following the Civil War. Even as formerly enslaved people rejoiced, white Texas legislators passed Black Codes that denied African Americans their **civil rights**, including the right to vote, hold office, or serve on juries.

As states across the South restricted the rights of African Americans, the U.S. Congress stepped in. Ten former Confederate states were placed under U.S. military control to ensure that African Americans were protected. This period is known as Reconstruction. By 1867, 25,000 U.S. troops were stationed in Texas to supervise new elections and the writing of a new state constitution. The 90 constitutional delegates included nine African Americans. The constitution they drew up provided for education for all children, equal legal rights for all, and help for the poor of both races.

African Americans had already moved to educate their children and themselves. With the help of organizations such as the federal government's Freedmen's Bureau, they had established 26 schools serving 1,600 students.

But some fought efforts to educate blacks. Many black schools with white teachers came under attack from racist groups such as the Ku Klux Klan. Immediately following the war, there was a wave of homicides in Texas, and most of the victims were black men, women, and children. In the first year after U.S. soldiers arrived to enforce the law, 500 men were charged with murdering blacks, but not one was convicted.

Reconstruction in Texas did not last long. Neither the U.S. Army nor the Texas state police, which included many black recruits, could halt white violence. African

WORD TO KNOW

civil rights *basic rights that are guaranteed to all Americans under the U.S. Constitution*

FAQ

Q: WHAT IS SHARECROPPING?

A: Sharecropping is a system of tenant farming that developed after the Civil War. A landowner provided a sharecropper with a plot of land to farm, along with seeds, tools, and other goods. The sharecropper raised the crops and then paid the landowner part of the value of the harvest as rent on the land. In reality, the landowners often overcharged the sharecroppers. Instead of receiving money at harvesttime, the sharecroppers ended up in debt to the landowners.

Americans in Texas concentrated on building churches, schools, and towns and advancing their children's education and economic opportunities. By 1872, whites had regained political power, and efforts at black progress ground to a halt. Many African Americans, along with some poor whites, were forced to become sharecroppers and ended up permanently in debt.

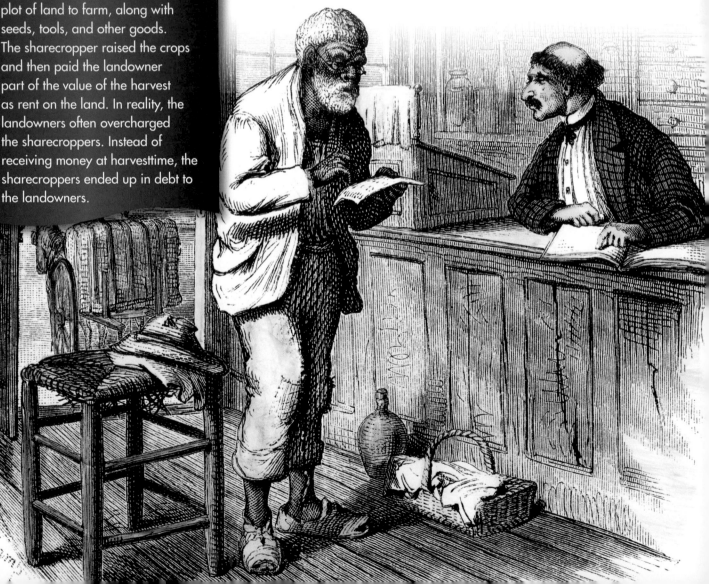

This farmer in 1870s Austin bargains for a price on his cotton.

Cowboys driving a herd of cattle from Texas to Kansas on the Chisholm Trail

ON THE CHISHOLM TRAIL

In Texas, raising cattle paid well. Cowboys got a horse to ride, food in their bellies, and $30 a month. Cowboys drove the cattle to Kansas, where they were loaded onto railroad cars. The Chisholm Trail led cattle out of Texas from 1867 to 1884. A steer that brought $14 in Texas was worth $100 in Kansas, so cattle drives were profitable. The Chisholm Trail, named for trader Jesse Chisholm, ran from South Texas through Austin all the way to Kansas. Over the years, millions of head of cattle were moved along the trail.

Moving 3,000 head of cattle required about a dozen men. A cook drove the chuck wagon, kept track of supplies, and prepared meals. It was the cook's job to make sure there was always a fresh pot of coffee on the campfire and plenty of grub for hungry cowboys. The cow-

MINI-BIO

BILL PICKETT: RODEO COWBOY

As a rodeo performer, Bill Pickett (1870–1932) wowed crowds at the 101 Ranch Wild West show and invented the technique of bulldogging (steer wrestling). Born in Travis County, Pickett had a mixed African American and Native American background. Sometimes he was banned from competing because of his skin color, but he appeared in some early films and became the first black cowboy movie star. He was named to the National Cowboy Hall of Fame in 1971.

? Want to know more? See www. famoustexans.com/billpickett.htm

Cowboys keeping watch over their herd at night during a cattle drive from Texas to Kansas

boys themselves were a mixed group—white, African American, Hispanic, and Native American. Experienced hands got to ride point, or at the head of the herd. New hands had to ride drag, or amid the dust cloud left behind by thousands of steers. The cowboys took turns during the night watching the herd.

Cattle drives faded as ranchers began moving their cattle on trains, but cowboys were still needed to work the ranches. About one-fourth of Texas cowboys were African American. Another 15 percent were Hispanic. The range was one place where race did not matter. Any cowboy who could handle a horse and a rope and do his share of the work earned respect.

VYING FOR LAND

Native Americans continued to resist white settlements after the Civil War. U.S. troops, many of them black, tried to keep the peace. Native Americans called these black troops Buffalo Soldiers, because their short, dark hair reminded them of buffalo. Some Buffalo Soldiers had American Indian ancestors. Although their main assignment was to stop Native American rebellions, many sympathized with the American Indians.

The open spaces of Texas—and the cheap cost of land—attracted many newcomers. The African American population in Texas doubled from 1860 to 1880 and nearly doubled again by 1900. But compared to the number of white people entering Texas at the time, the ratio of blacks to whites was actually decreasing. Many African Americans moved to Texas after the Civil War seeking cheap land and independence. Some joined American Indian nations.

Many white people arrived from other Southern states, while others came from foreign countries. Germans were the largest immigrant group to enter, but Irish, French, English, Czechs, and Swedes also settled in the state. During the great waves of immigration from 1846 to 1915, Galveston was second only to New York City as an entry point for Europeans. For some, Texas was a place where you could reinvent yourself—and perhaps strike it rich.

MINI-BIO

QUANAH PARKER: THE LAST COMANCHE CHIEF

Quanah Parker (1850–1911) was the son of Comanche chief Peta Nocona and Cynthia Parker, a white woman captured in a raid in 1836. Quanah Parker was the last Comanche chief, and he never lost a battle to the white soldiers. His community was the last on the Llano Estacado to sign a treaty and agree to live on a reservation. Parker later became a judge on the reservation and worked with the U.S. Congress on behalf of the Comanche people.

? Want to know more? See www.tsha.utexas.edu/handbook/online/articles/PP/fpa28.html

Buffalo Soldier

A crowd watches
a gusher at
Spindletop, in
Beaumont, the
site of the state's
first oil discovery,
in January 1901.

1901

*Oil is discovered
at Spindletop*

◄ 1925

*"Ma" Ferguson
becomes Texas's first
female governor*

1929

*The Great
Depression begins*

C H A P T E R   F I V E

MORE MODERN TIMES

★

O N JANUARY 10, 1901, MUD, GAS, AND OIL ERUPTED FROM A WELL AT SPINDLETOP. It was this spurt of oil, more than any other event, that thrust Texas into the industrial age. Spindletop attracted fortune hunters to oil drilling in the same way that gold drew miners to California during the gold rush. Oil—nicknamed Texas tea—promised long-term wealth for many Texans.

1941
The United States enters World War II

1964 ▸
Lyndon Johnson signs the Civil Rights Act

2005
Refugees from Hurricane Katrina pour into Texas

Workers loading bales of cotton onto railcars, around 1906

SEE IT HERE!

EAST TEXAS OIL MUSEUM

The oil industry brought a new way of life to Texas in the 1930s. Some people became rich; some lost everything. Men and women dared to dream that wells would make their fortunes. Learn all about oil drilling, wildcatting, and wells pinchin' out at the East Texas Oil Museum on the Kilgore College campus in Kilgore. Boom or bust— you'll have a great time.

KING COTTON AND TEXAS TEA

Cotton dominated Texas agriculture as the 1900s began. Landowners collected huge profits, while sharecroppers lived in poverty. In 1892, a beetle called the boll weevil had begun moving from Mexico into the United States. The tiny weevil laid its eggs in cotton bolls, or pods, and its larvae feasted on the cotton as they grew. Over time, the weevils devoured millions of dollars in cotton crops. Although cotton production eventually rebounded, by the 1920s, cotton was again in trouble as prices fell below 10 cents a pound.

At the same time, rural Texas was changing. Small farms gave way to giant ranches covering hundreds of thousands of acres. Commercial grain farming increased as trains made it easy to get wheat, oats, sorghum, and corn to market. Lumbering and flour milling industries blossomed. Meanwhile, as more people bought cars, trucks, and farm vehicles, oil profits soared.

THE GREAT DEPRESSION

On October 29, 1929, the New York Stock Exchange suffered its worst day on record. In a few weeks, the value of **stocks** had fallen by 40 percent. The stock market crash ruined many banks. As banks failed, so did businesses. The United States tumbled into the Great Depression.

Millions of people lost their jobs. Without work, fewer people bought cars, which reduced Texas's gasoline sales. People bought less Texas beef at the butcher shop and fewer towels and sheets made from Texas cotton. Then Mother Nature unleashed a long drought. Cotton and wheat fields dried up, and the soil blew away in what was called the Dust Bowl. Farmers had few crops to sell and no buyers. Many lost their farms. Men and boys left home to seek work. Families stood in lines at soup kitchens to get meals. People who lost their homes began to live in shacks in makeshift towns, named Hoovervilles after President Herbert Hoover.

In 1932, Franklin D. Roosevelt won the presidential election (with Texan John Nance Garner as his vice president) by proposing a relief program called the New Deal. Part of the New Deal was a jobs program called the Works Progress Administration (WPA).

MINI-BIO

"MA" FERGUSON: GOING HER OWN WAY

Miriam "Ma" Ferguson (1875–1961) ran for governor for the first time in 1924. Her husband, James "Pa" Ferguson, had once been governor but was now banned from running for office because he was a crook. Ma won the election and became Texas's first woman governor. As governor, she condemned the Ku Klux Klan. She also issued more than 2,000 pardons to state prisoners in her first two years in office. After two years, Texas had had enough of Ma Ferguson. She lost the next election, though in 1932, she won a second term as governor.

? Want to know more? See www.tshaonline.org/handbook/online/articles/FF/ffe6.html

---

WORD TO KNOW

stocks *shares in the ownership of a company*

Under the WPA, 600,000 Texans went to work on a variety of construction, education, and history projects. Archaeologists uncovered Native American villages. Construction workers built bridges, schools, hospitals, and preschool play centers.

From 1933 to 1943, artists working for the WPA painted 97 murals in 66 Texas post offices. Howard Cook's *San Antonio's Importance in Texas History* is considered one of the best murals. Another New Deal program, the Civilian Conservation Corps (CCC), put people to work in 15 state parks. At Bastrop State Park, the CCC built roads, cabins, and picnic shelters.

People wait in line to receive food and other supplies from a San Antonio relief program during the Great Depression.

WORLD WAR II

As hard as Roosevelt worked to end the Depression, it was actually World War II (1939–1945) that put Americans back to work full-time. World War II began in 1939, when Germany invaded Poland. The war soon spread across Europe. At the same time, Japan was invading other countries in Asia. In 1941, after a surprise Japanese attack on the U.S. naval base at Pearl Harbor, in the Hawaiian Islands, the United States entered the war. Texan Chester Nimitz led the navy fleet in the Pacific against the Japanese. Thousands of Texans joined the military.

The war effort revived the Texas economy. Shipyards sprang up in Beaumont, Port Arthur, Houston, Galveston, and Corpus Christi. Steel mills in Houston and Fort Worth worked around the clock. Texas wheat helped feed soldiers and hungry people in Europe.

The war changed life in Texas. While men fought overseas, women became plumbers, electricians, and welders. They ran farms and factories. Before World War II, women mostly worked in the home. After the war, many women did not want to return to the kitchen. Around the same time, half a million people moved to the cities, changing Texas from a rural to a largely urban state.

Women in Fort Worth assembling a C-87 transport plane in 1942

THE CIVIL RIGHTS MOVEMENT

When the war ended, hundreds of thousands of veterans returned home to Texas. Many wanted their old jobs back, but others wanted more than that. African American veterans had earned respect for their sacrifices and contributions to the war effort. In Texas, however, black veterans were still treated poorly. **Segregation** was the law of the land. Black people could not attend the same schools as whites. They could not shop in white stores or live in white neighborhoods. Unfair laws also hurt Mexican Americans. Facing persistent discrimination, black and Hispanic Texans sought to change their lives.

African Americans joined the NAACP (National Association for the Advancement of Colored People), and Latinos formed LULAC (League of United Latin American Citizens), an organization that fights for equal rights. In 1954, the U.S. Supreme Court ruled in *Brown v. Board of Education* that segregated schools were illegal. Yet some white Texans refused to end segregation. In 1956, Governor R. Allan Shivers called out the Texas Rangers to stop black students from attending white schools in Mansfield. The struggle continued through the early 1960s. Finally, after many public protests, Texas schools were desegregated.

On November 22, 1963, President John F. Kennedy was

MINI-BIO

JOSÉ ANGEL GUTIÉRREZ: WORKING FOR CHANGE

José Angel Gutiérrez (1944–) grew up in Crystal City, in South Texas. As a young man in the 1960s, he founded the Mexican American Youth Organization and La Raza Unida Party, a Hispanic political party. Gutiérrez later founded the Center for Mexican American Studies at the University of Texas at Arlington and became an attorney. He was named one of the 100 Outstanding Latino Texans of the 20th Century. He continues to urge Mexican Americans to take an active role in solving the problems in their communities and the nation.

 Want to know more? See www.uta.edu/public-affairs/statements/gutierrez2.html

President Lyndon B. Johnson (seated) shakes hands with Martin Luther King Jr. at the signing of the Civil Rights Act on July 2, 1964.

assassinated in Dallas. This event stunned the nation and the world. Within hours, Lee Harvey Oswald was arrested for murder. Two days later, Oswald was shot and killed while in police custody.

Following Kennedy's murder, Vice President Lyndon B. Johnson, a Texan, became president. Under Johnson's leadership, the U.S. Congress passed the Civil Rights Act of 1964, outlawing discrimination based on race, color, religion, sex, or national origin. Johnson proudly signed the bill into law in the presence of major civil rights leaders such as Martin Luther King Jr. In 1965, Johnson signed the Voting Rights Act, which outlawed discriminatory restrictions on voting.

A massive effort to enroll minority voters brought many African Americans and Hispanics to the polls. In 1966, Barbara Jordan became the first African American to serve in the state senate since Reconstruction. She later went on to become a member of the U.S. House of Representatives. Two other African Americans—Curtis Graves of Houston and Joe Lockridge of Dallas—also won seats in the state house of representatives. In 1963 and again in 1969, Mexican Americans in Crystal City

MINI-BIO

BARBARA JORDAN: SERVING TEXAS

One of Texas's most significant lawmakers was Barbara Jordan (1936–1996). Born in Houston, she was elected to the state senate in 1966. She was the first African American to serve in the state senate since 1883. In 1967, she became its presiding officer. Jordan won election to the U.S. House of Representatives in 1973. As a congresswoman, she championed the poor, African Americans, and other underserved people. She left politics in 1979 and became a professor at the Lyndon Baines Johnson School of Public Affairs, but she remained a powerful voice of compassion.

❓ **Want to know more?** See www.tshaonline.org/handbook/online/articles/JJ/fjoas.html

battled the tradition of whites running both city hall and Crystal City public schools. Five Hispanic candidates ran for city council—and all five won.

PROSPERITY, SCANDAL, AND A HELPING HAND

After the civil unrest of the 1950s and 1960s, Texas settled into a period of peace and prosperity. The oil and gas industry earned record profits in the second half of the 20th century. The NASA space program at Houston became a center for the aerospace industry.

A stock fraud scandal in Sharpstown rocked the state in 1971 and 1972. Nearly two dozen state officials were charged and

Workers in NASA's mission control room in Houston monitor the *Gemini V* spaceflight in 1962.

found guilty of trading their votes in the Texas legislature for stocks.

By the end of the 20th century, the population of Texas was increasing dramatically as many people moved to the state in search of jobs and a warm climate. Then, in 2005, Hurricane Katrina hit the Gulf Coast, devastating the region. In the aftermath of the hurricane, nearly 240,000 refugees fled to Texas, particularly Houston. Most had been flooded out of their homes in New Orleans, Louisiana. The influx of people in need strained public services. But Texans pride themselves on being friendly, and many were ready to lend a helping hand.

Survivors of Hurricane Katrina taking shelter in Houston's Astrodome

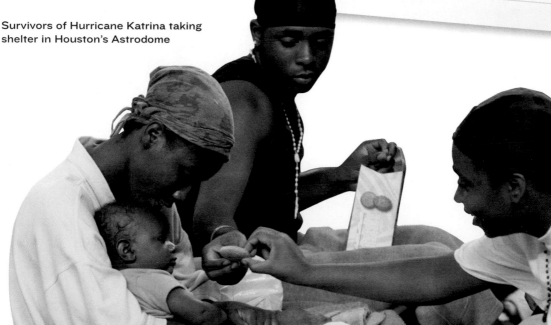

READ ABOUT

Sightseers and
diners enjoy a
day at Riverwalk
in San Antonio.

PEOPLE

★

IN THE EL PASO FARMERS MARKET, VISITORS LINE UP FOR TAMALES AND OVERSTUFFED BURRITOS. In Port Arthur, Cajun restaurants turn out steaming bowls of jambalaya and gumbo. Up in the Hill Country, they're scrving bratwurst or sauerbraten. In an Amarillo diner, chicken-fried steak and gravy is today's special. And there's barbecue to be relished just about everywhere. Different foods, different folks, different traditions—and it's all Texas.

THE PEOPLE OF TEXAS

In 1900, most Texans lived on farms or ranches. By 2000, the majority lived in cities. Why the big shift? One reason was that corporations had taken over most farms from families. People moved to the city to find jobs.

Houston, San Antonio, and Dallas each have populations of more than 1 million. Another 25 Texas cities are home to 100,000 people or more. Of Texas's nearly 24 million people, about half are white, a little more than one-third are Hispanic, around one-tenth are African American, and the rest are Native American or Asian/Pacific Islanders.

Anglos trace their heritage back to non-Spanish Europe. Many Irish people arrived after the Republic of Texas was formed in 1836. They brought traditions of fiddle playing, singing, and dancing. German settle-

High school marching bands and other parade participants gather to celebrate Juneteenth in Austin.

71

Students in Freeport taking part in a Cinco de Mayo celebration

ments in Texas brought foods such as bratwurst and sauerkraut. In German music halls, polkas fill the air and stomping feet shake the floorboards. Another prominent group, the Cajuns, trace their families back to the French Acadian settlers in Canada. The Acadians moved to New Orleans and spread westward into Texas. The Cajuns' blend of accordion and guitar music can be heard in East Texas dance halls on Saturday nights.

Mexico lost its land in the Texas Revolution, but it left a lasting culture. Spanish influence in Texas began with the missions and continues in the architecture of ranches and Catholic churches. Mexican American mariachi bands strum their guitars in restaurants and public parks. On Cinco de Mayo (May 5), which commemorates a victory by Mexican forces in 1862, every Texan is Mexican. They attend parades, barbecues, and fiestas.

FAQ

Q: WHERE DOES TEXAS'S POPULATION RANK IN THE UNITED STATES?

A: In 2000, Texas had a population of 20,851,820. Its population ranks second among the states, trailing only California.

Where Texans Live

The colors on this map indicate population density throughout the state. The darker the color, the more people live there.

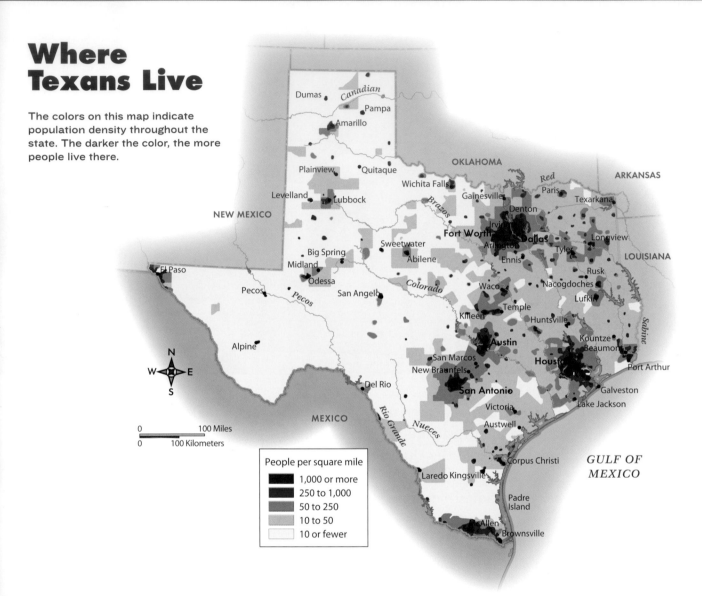

People per square mile

■	1,000 or more
■	250 to 1,000
■	50 to 250
■	10 to 50
□	10 or fewer

The first Africans came to Texas aboard Spanish ships, as enslaved workers and servants. Later, enslaved Africans worked on Texas plantations. Free blacks arrived in the early days of the Republic, becoming ranchers and landowners. After the Civil War, Africans came to Texas seeking cheap land and independence.

Texas is home to 65,000 Native Americans, the sixth-highest total of any state. Few live on reservations.

COUNTRY AND CITY

Texas is a place that gives meaning to the phrase "wide-open spaces." Life in small towns revolves around farming. People either are farmers or provide services to farm families. Many teens work at least part-time on the family farm and take part in 4-H. Pickup trucks are common, and many youngsters on farms learn to drive a tractor before they drive the family car

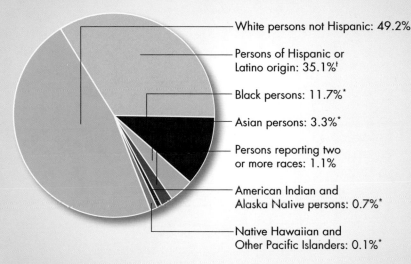

People QuickFacts

White persons not Hispanic: 49.2%

Persons of Hispanic or Latino origin: 35.1%[t]

Black persons: 11.7%[*]

Asian persons: 3.3%[*]

Persons reporting two or more races: 1.1%

American Indian and Alaska Native persons: 0.7%[*]

Native Hawaiian and Other Pacific Islanders: 0.1%[*]

*Hispanics may be of any race, so they also are included in applicable race categories
[t]Includes persons reporting only one race
Source: U.S. Census Bureau, 2005

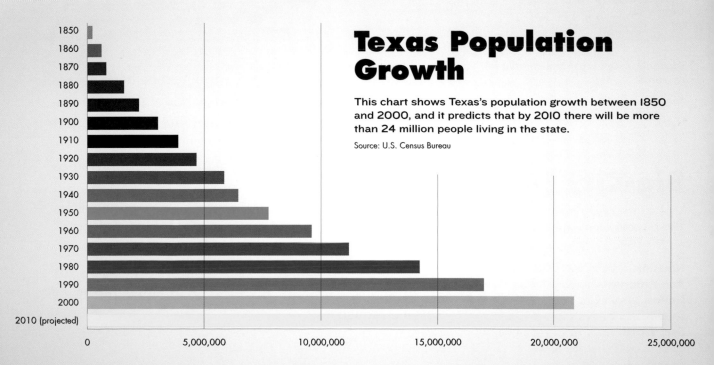

Texas Population Growth

This chart shows Texas's population growth between 1850 and 2000, and it predicts that by 2010 there will be more than 24 million people living in the state.

Source: U.S. Census Bureau

Students in Texas use the Internet for research.

Big-City Life

This list shows the population of Texas's biggest cities.

Houston	2,016,582
San Antonio	1,256,509
Dallas	1,213,825
Austin	690,252
Fort Worth	624,067

Source: U.S. Census Bureau, 2006 estimate

Like people everywhere, rural Texans have access to instant communications, news, shopping, and entertainment through the Internet, satellite television, and phones.

In Texas's cities, families live in single-family homes or apartment buildings. Life moves at a faster pace, and traffic is part of that lifestyle. The state's major cities are sprawling urban centers connected by multilane highways. City workers rise early, drive to work, and spend their days in high-rise buildings, factories, or small shops. They are involved in manufacturing or service industries.

EDUCATION

More than 4.5 million children in Texas attend public school. All public school programs meet TEKS—Texas Essential Knowledge and Skills—standards. Students take standardized tests in reading, writing, English, language arts, math, science, and social studies, depending on their grade levels.

Students can continue their education at community colleges, public and private colleges, and universities. The University of Texas at Austin has the fifth-largest academic library in the United States. The school has 50,000 students. Rice University, one of the nation's top private colleges, is small by comparison, with only 3,000 undergraduate students. Its science program is highly regarded. Texas A&M University programs emphasize agriculture, mining, life sciences, engineering, and political science.

Students walk across campus at the University of Texas at Austin.

HOW TO TALK LIKE A TEXAN

Include these phrases in your vocabulary, and you'll fit in from Dallas to Dilley and all around Texas.

blue norther	a storm that develops as a giant, blue-black cloud of cold air, comes over the warm gulf air, and "just about freezes us to death"
catty whompus	something that doesn't quite fit properly or is out of line
'fess up	confess, admit
frog-strangler	an extraordinary amount of rain
Panhandle rain	a dust storm
to have conniptions	to get upset and cause a ruckus
walking in tall cotton	doing fine

HOW TO EAT LIKE A TEXAN

Take traditional Mexican foods, add a Texas twist, and you've got Tex-Mex cuisine. Typical Tex-Mex dishes include nachos and tacos. They are spicier than most American dishes and milder than some Mexican foods.

Along the coast, expect to find fresh shrimp, oysters, blue crabs, and red snapper on the menu. These saltwater creatures are plucked from the Gulf of Mexico in the morning and make it to restaurant menus by dinner.

Throughout Texas, barbecue brings friends together and creates lively debate. The arguments about barbecue include the type of wood burned, the spices used, and the sauce provided. Most Texans prefer mesquite coals, although those in the apple-growing regions swear by applewood. What meat should be used? The most common choice is beef, although pork is a favorite for some people.

Tex-Mex nachos

MENU

WHAT'S ON THE MENU IN TEXAS?

★ ★ ★

Chicken-Fried Steak

This is the unofficial state dish of Texas. It is a steak, breaded in seasoned flour or bread crumbs and fried, then slathered in a pool of gravy.

Huevos Rancheros

This traditional Mexican breakfast is now popular across Texas. Spice up your eggs with hot peppers and serve them with beans, salsa, and tortillas for a satisfying meal.

Sweet Onions

Texas sweet onions originally came from the Bermuda Islands in 1898. Since then, Texas has grown these sweet bulbs by the ton. Eat them raw, fried, grilled, or baked—Texas sweets bring fewer tears and bigger smiles to the dinner table.

Biscuits and Gravy

Take the drippings from frying sausages and make gravy from it. Open up a couple of flaky biscuits and pour on that sausage gravy. The result is a breakfast dish that Texans rave about.

Biscuits and gravy

TRY THIS RECIPE
Texas Chili

In 1902, William Gebhardt of New Braunfels invented chili powder. Texans like their chili hot! Try this version, but have an adult nearby to help.

Ingredients:
2 tablespoons olive oil
5 cloves garlic, minced
2 onions, diced
1½ pounds ground beef
salt and pepper to taste
2 tablespoons red chili powder
4 plum tomatoes, blanched, peeled, and diced
½ cup tomato paste
2 cups beef stock
¾ teaspoon ground cumin
2 teaspoons oregano
¼ cup parsley, minced, fresh

Instructions:
1. Heat the oil in a large saucepan.
2. Add the garlic and onions and sauté over medium-high heat for 5 minutes.
3. Add the beef, stirring frequently, until all the beef is browned. Drain off the excess fat.
4. Season the meat with salt and pepper, stir in the chili powder, and cook for 2 minutes.
5. Add the tomatoes, tomato paste, beef stock, cumin, oregano, and parsley and stir.
6. Bring to a simmer, turn down the heat, and cook, covered, for 60 minutes. Stir occasionally.
7. Ladle into bowls and enjoy.

Willie Nelson helped introduce Austin-style music to audiences outside Texas.

MAKING MUSIC

Texas's music tradition began with Mexican *corridos*, songs that easily translated into cowboy songs and country-and-western ballads. Texan music also developed with some Anglo influences, often using stringed instruments such as the fiddle. German and other European immigrants brought accordions to the Texas region in the 19th century, and Mexican Texans gradually incorporated these sounds into their own musical styles. The country ballad eventually evolved, in part, from Anglo musical traditions.

Since then, Texans have been making major contributions to music. In the 1930s and 1940s, Bob Wills, who was born near Kosse, led the Texas Playboys band. Today, Austin is Texas's music capital, and the PBS television program *Austin City Limits* has featured most major country stars. Texas natives Willie Nelson and Waylon Jennings brought Austin-style country-and-western music to national attention, a tradition that is carried on by many Texas bands, including the Dixie Chicks. Rock-and-roll pioneer Buddy Holly was born in Lubbock and later influenced bands such as The Beatles and The Rolling Stones. Country and pop singer Mac Davis also hailed from Lubbock.

Many musicians believe that the blues came about from field chants, songs sung by enslaved workers in the South. A number of Texas musicians adopted the blues as their musical style. Among the greatest Texas blues artists was Blind Lemon Jefferson, who wrote such classics as "Matchbox Blues" and "Black Snake Moan." Other Texas blues greats include Alger "Texas" Alexander, T-Bone Walker, and Blind Willie Johnson.

Conjunto is a type of Mexican American dance music. Conjunto bands include an accordion, drums, and a 12-string bass guitar. The rhythm is based on traditional polka music. As early as 1935, conjunto music by Narciso Martinez was being played throughout Texas. Today, conjunto is heard at fairs, concerts, and clubs. Tejano music is a variety of conjunto with blues and country influences. Mariachi bands often produce romantic music at weddings and other events. Mariachi bands usually include violins, trumpets, small guitars, and a bass.

MINI-BIO

SELENA: QUEEN OF TEJANO

Selena (1971–1995) was a native of Lake Jackson, Texas. Born Selena Quintanilla-Perez, she was considered the Queen of Tejano, a type of Mexican music that mixed in other styles, such as country. Selena began performing as a child. By age 10, she was the lead singer in her family's band, Selena y los Dinos. She won Female Vocalist of the Year and Performer of the Year at the 1987 Tejano Music Awards. Her career came to an early end when she was murdered, but fans of Tejano continue to love her music.

? Want to know more? See www.tshaonline. org/handbook/online/articles/QQ/fquxg.html

Frederic Remington painting in his studio in 1891

MINI-BIO

SANDRA CISNEROS: AUTHOR AND POET

Sandra Cisneros (1954—) grew up in a poor Mexican American neighborhood. She has created memorable portraits of that world in books such as *The House on Mango Street* and *Woman Hollering Creek and Other Stories*. Cisneros often writes about difficult, painful issues because she believes it is important to expose such stories. She has won two National Endowment for the Arts awards, as well as a MacArthur Foundation Fellowship. She lives in San Antonio.

 Want to know more?
See www.sandracisneros.com

ART AND WRITING

George Catlin memorialized Texas's Native American cultures in paintings of the Caddos and Comanches. Mexican vaqueros, the earliest cowboys, were popular subjects for artwork. As Anglo cowboys joined Mexican vaqueros, cowboy art became popular throughout the United States. Late in the 1800s, paintings and sculptures by Frederic Remington and Charles Russell created lasting scenes of cattle drives, cowboys, and Native Americans.

Cowboys, ranching, and oil drilling are also common themes among many Texas writers. Katherine Anne Porter wrote short stories set in her native central Texas and won both the Pulitzer Prize and the National

Book Award for her *Collected Stories*. The son and grandson of Texas ranchers, Larry McMurtry writes realistic and compelling Western novels. Jovita González delved into her own Mexican American background when she wrote her stories and songs. She was particularly interested in Mexican American folklore. Sandra Cisneros, a novelist and poet from San Antonio, also writes stories set in Mexican American neighborhoods.

Poet, author, and teacher Tómas Rivera hailed from Crystal City. His works include the novel *And the Earth Did Not Part* and a book of poetry, *Always and Other Poems*. Naomi Shihab Nye writes poems, children's books, and songs that draw on her own Arab American heritage and traditions of her Texas neighbors. Louis Sachar, an Austin-based children's writer, has written many books, including *Holes*, which won a Newbery Medal. *Holes* concerns a young boy who gets in trouble and ends up in a Texas detention camp. The children there are forced to dig holes, but they also hear plenty of Texas lore.

MINI-BIO

NAOMI SHIHAB NYE: "WANDERING POET"

Children's author Naomi Shihab Nye (1952–) writes poems and stories that deal with her Mexican American neighbors and her Arab American background. Her young adult novel *Habibi* tells the story of an Arab American teenager who moves to the Middle East. Nye has won many awards for her work, including the Jane Addams Children's Book Award and the Paterson Poetry Prize. She has sometimes referred to herself as a "wandering poet," but she calls San Antonio home.

? Want to know more? See www. poetryfoundation.org/archive/poet.html?id=5053

Louis Sachar won the Newbery Medal for his novel *Holes*.

SPORTS

Football is as much a part of Texas as cattle and oil. In towns across the state, the high school football stadium is the place to be on Friday nights in the fall. High school football is more than a sport—it's family, friends, and fierce fans.

Texas hosts many professional sports teams. The Dallas Cowboys and the Houston Texans compete in the National Football League. The Dallas Mavericks, the San Antonio Spurs, and the Houston Rockets play in the National Basketball Association, while the Houston Comets and the San Antonio Silver Stars are part of the Women's National Basketball Association. Baseball fans in Houston

MINI-BIO

"BABE" DIDRIKSON ZAHARIAS: OLYMPIC CHAMPION

Mildred Ella "Babe" Didrikson Zaharias (1911–1956), a native of Port Arthur, was one of the best all-around athletes in history. As a child, Zaharias excelled in several sports, including baseball. In fact, she was so good that she earned the nickname "Babe" after Babe Ruth. She won two Olympic gold medals in track-and-field events in 1932, played baseball, and won 55 pro and amateur golf events. She helped found the Ladies Professional Golf Association (LPGA) and was voted the greatest female athlete of the first half of the 20th century by the Associated Press. She remains one of the most significant figures in women's sports history.

? **Want to know more?** See www.babedidriksonzaharias.org/

Silver Stars teammates celebrate a victory.

Houston Texans fans cheer as their team takes the field.

come out to watch the Astros, while in Arlington, near Dallas, fans cheer on the Texas Rangers. Meanwhile, FC Dallas heats up the soccer fields, while the Dallas Stars hit slap shots into the goal in professional hockey games.

Texas has produced many world-class athletes. Track-and-field stars Michael Johnson and Darold Williamson are both native Texans. George Foreman won Olympic gold in boxing, and Del Rio, Texas, has produced a top bobsled driver in Todd Hays. In the world of cycling, no one has been as successful as seven-time Tour de France champion Lance Armstrong.

MINI-BIO

LEE TREVINO: GOLFING CHAMPION

Lee Trevino (1939–) was born into a poor Mexican American family in Dallas. When he was young, his uncle gave him some old golf balls and one battered golf club. Soon, Trevino was spending every spare moment whacking the balls. Poverty pushed him out of school after eighth grade so he could work full time. He worked as a golf caddy, and by practicing every day after work, he became a great golfer. He was the first Mexican American to win the Masters, the U.S. Open, the British Open, and the PGA Championship. In 1981, he was inducted into the World Golf Hall of Fame. Trevino continues to play golf and serves as a role model for young Mexican American athletes.

? **Want to know more?** See www.wghof.org/hof/member.php?member=1116

READ ABOUT

While touring the state capitol, visitors pause on the Republic of Texas mosaic on the rotunda floor.

CHAPTER SEVEN

GOVERNMENT

★

SINCE THE SPANISH FIRST ARRIVED IN THE REGION, NUMEROUS FLAGS HAVE FLOWN OVER TEXAS. The first was Spain's red-and-gold banner. The fleur-de-lis flower design of France and the red, white, and green of Mexico were next. The Republic of Texas became independent under the Lone Star Flag. When Texas joined the Union, the Stars and Stripes was run up the flagpole. A Confederate flag flew in Texas during the Civil War. Each flag represents part of the state's heritage. Today, the Lone Star Flag proudly waves as the state flag.

Capitol Facts

Here are some interesting facts about Texas's state capitol.

Height of dome . . . . 311 feet
(95 m), which is 7 feet (2 m) taller
than the dome of the Capitol in
Washington, D.C.
Length . . . . 566.5 feet (172.7 m)
Completed 1882
Cost $3,744,600

The Texas capitol is the country's largest state capitol building.

The state capitol in Austin

THE CAPITOL

The center of Texas government is the capitol. The governor, senators, and representatives, and the people who work for them, have offices and meeting rooms in the capitol. Today's building came about in an odd way. A fire destroyed the old capitol in 1881, and lawmakers decided to hold a contest to find an architect for the new building. Ads appeared in newspapers nationwide. The winning design was modeled after the Capitol in Washington, D.C.

Government officials wanted all the materials used in the capitol to be from Texas. One thousand construction workers used 4,000 train carloads of red granite and 11,000 carloads of limestone to make the building. The lumber they used would measure 7 miles (11 km) laid end to end. The roof took 85,000 square feet (7,900 sq m) of copper. When complete, the building had 392 rooms, 924 windows, and 404 doors.

Capital City

This map shows places of interest in
Austin, Texas's capital city.

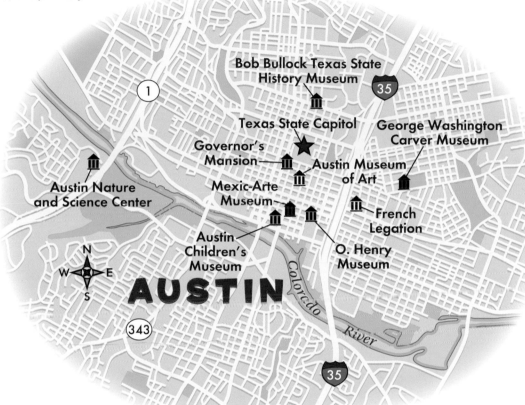

THE EXECUTIVE BRANCH

A drought strikes, and cattle feed becomes scarce.
Without food, the cattle may die. In 1998, the Texas
Department of Agriculture answered this problem
by setting up a "hay hotline." Farmers who have hay
or other cattle feed can list their product and phone
number on a Web site. Ranchers who need hay can call
and make arrangements for pickup or delivery. This is
just one example of the many problems solved by the
executive branch of the Texas government.

Texas's State Government

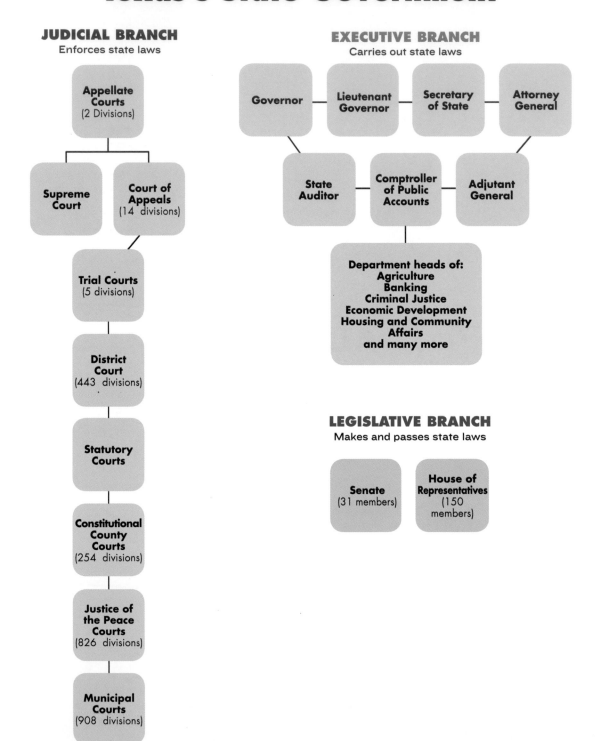

JUDICIAL BRANCH
Enforces state laws

Appellate Courts
(2 Divisions)

Supreme Court

Court of Appeals
(14 divisions)

Trial Courts
(5 divisions)

District Court
(443 divisions)

Statutory Courts

Constitutional County Courts
(254 divisions)

Justice of the Peace Courts
(826 divisions)

Municipal Courts
(908 divisions)

EXECUTIVE BRANCH
Carries out state laws

Governor

Lieutenant Governor

Secretary of State

Attorney General

State Auditor

Comptroller of Public Accounts

Adjutant General

Department heads of:
Agriculture
Banking
Criminal Justice
Economic Development
Housing and Community Affairs
and many more

LEGISLATIVE BRANCH
Makes and passes state laws

Senate
(31 members)

House of Representatives
(150 members)

The executive branch includes the governor, the lieutenant governor, the attorney general, the comptroller of public accounts, the secretary of state, and varied agencies such as the Department of Agriculture, the General Land Office, the Department of Family and Protective Services, and the Texas Music Office.

Texas elects its governor every four years. To be governor, the candidate must be at least 30 years old and a resident of Texas for five years immediately before the election. It is the governor's job to recommend policies or new laws to lawmakers. The governor signs bills into law. He or she can also veto a bill to reject it. If a judge has left office, the governor appoints a replacement. The governor also deals with issues involving education, safety, prisons, highways, taxes, and establishing new state parks. Committee or department heads study problems and recommend actions to the governor.

The primary duty of the lieutenant governor is presiding over the state senate. He or she votes only if there is a tie. The lieutenant governor also steps in if the governor cannot continue to serve. The attorney general's office represents Texas's interests in court. The comptroller's office oversees collecting state tax money and keeping

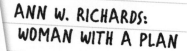

MINI-BIO

ANN W. RICHARDS: WOMAN WITH A PLAN

Ann Richards (1933–2006), who was born in Lakeview, had an interest in politics from a young age. By the mid-1970s, she was elected a county commissioner in Austin. Her lively sense of humor and tough-mindedness helped her rise through the political ranks. In 1982, she was elected state treasurer, becoming the first woman to win statewide office in Texas in 50 years. When she became governor of Texas in 1991, she had a plan to revive the state's struggling economy. She promoted government efficiency by checking on every department yearly. Richards also appointed many women and minorities to important state offices. Today, her larger-than-life persona lives on in the memory of many Texans.

? **Want to know more?** See www.tsl.state.tx.us/governors/modern/richards-p01.html

WORDS TO KNOW

marketing *the business of presenting products and services for sale to potential customers*

foster care *a government-run system of housing and caring for neglected or orphaned children*

probation *a time during which a person convicted of a crime is evaluated*

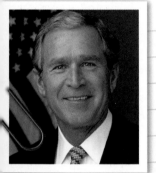

MINI-BIO

GEORGE W. BUSH: GOVERNOR AND PRESIDENT

George W. Bush (1946–) was born in Connecticut but grew up in Midland and Houston. Following a career in the oil business, he entered politics and was elected governor of Texas in 1994. He was reelected in 1998. The son of President George H. W. Bush, he won the 2000 presidential election and was reelected in 2004. As the 43rd president of the United States, Bush led the United States in military actions in Afghanistan and Iraq as part of the "war on terror."

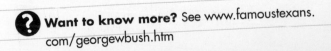

❓ **Want to know more?** See www.famoustexans.com/georgewbush.htm

track of how the state spends that money. The secretary of state keeps records about state business, publishes state statistics, and runs state elections.

The Department of Agriculture and the General Land Office both deal with land and its use. The Department of Agriculture controls the **marketing** of the state's major agricultural products. The office also provides information about pest control and regulations regarding raising livestock or produce. The General Land Office takes care of public lands and manages state office buildings, public schools, and parks.

The Texas Youth Connection, a section of the Department of Family Protective Services, offers online advice for parents and children. In particular, many children in **foster care** need help when they reach adulthood, and this Web site offers information about education, studying, applying to college, and getting scholarships. The department provides financial advice for young people. Information on finding and getting health or dental care, safety issues, and nutrition fill the Health section. The Web site even teaches teens how to cook, and how to shop for groceries.

THE JUDICIAL BRANCH

A 15-year-old boy is arrested for shoplifting. The police call the child's parents, who come to the police station to talk about the crime. Although this is a serious crime, it does not require jail as a punishment. The court sentences the boy to two years' **probation**. Once a week, he must check in with his probation officer. The officer checks that the boy goes to school regularly, behaves well in school, and is home every night by curfew. Every two weeks, the family will go to counseling. In addition, the judge sentences the boy to 50 hours of community service. In this case, the boy will work three hours each Saturday morning at a local soup kitchen.

Texas courts deal with problems ranging from teenage shoplifters to divorces to murder. Justice courts and municipal courts deal with minor crimes and small civil cases. Typical cases might deal with suing a business or reckless driving. County courts hear cases about juvenile crimes, wills, and small lawsuits. The 443 district courts in Texas handle civil and criminal cases. Criminal cases include crimes such as armed robbery or embezzling (stealing) corporate funds.

WEIRD AND WACKY LAWS

Texas has some pretty weird laws. Can you believe these are on the books?

- It is illegal for children to have unusual haircuts.
- Criminals must give their victims 24 hours' notice, either orally or in writing, and explain the nature of the crime about to be committed.
- It is illegal to milk another person's cow.
- In Houston, it is illegal to sell Limburger cheese on Sunday.
- It's illegal to put graffiti on someone else's cow.

Texas has **443 district courts,** which hold trials for civil and criminal cases.

A view of the Texas House of
Representatives in session

The upper courts in Texas are the courts of appeals, the court of criminal appeals, and the Texas Supreme Court. Someone who thinks a mistake was made during a trial can ask a court of appeals to review the case. There are 14 courts and 80 justices in the courts of appeals. When an appeal is made, five justices listen to the arguments and decide whether the earlier trial or judgment was fair. For serious crimes, appeals might go straight to the court of criminal appeals, which has nine justices. They have the last say in a criminal case. The last say in a civil case lies with the supreme court, which also has nine justices. Citizens elect judges and justices, who serve terms of four years in lower courts and six years in upper courts.

WORD TO KNOW

revenue *taxes and other income collected by a government*

THE LEGISLATIVE BRANCH

The Texas legislature is made up of two houses: the senate and the house of representatives. Both houses are charged with writing laws, but in some cases their responsibilities are different. All bills that deal with state **revenue** must begin in the house of representatives. And only the senate approves officials appointed by the governor.

Representing Texas

This list shows the number of elected officials who represent Texas, both on state and national levels.

OFFICE	NUMBER	LENGTH OF TERM
State representatives	150	2 years
State senators	31	4 years
U.S. representatives	32	2 years
U.S. senators	2	6 years
Presidential electors	34	—

The state senate has 31 senators. Senators must be at least 26 years old and have been a Texas citizen for at least five years before the election. They must also have lived in the district they will represent for at least a year. Senators serve four-year terms, and half of the senate runs for election every two years.

The state house of representatives has 150 members, and they run for election every two years. Representatives must be 21 years old and a Texas citizen for at least two years. Like senators, candidates must have lived in the districts they represent for at least a year before the election.

Governor Rick Perry addresses the state house of representatives in 2007.

TEXAS PRESIDENTS

Dwight D. Eisenhower (1890–1969) was born in Denison and served as president from 1953 to 1961.

Lyndon B. Johnson (1908–1973) became president when John F. Kennedy was assassinated in Dallas in 1963. A native of Stonewall, he was president from 1963 to 1969.

George H. W. Bush (1924–) served as president from 1989 to 1993. Bush grew up in Connecticut and then moved to Texas to work in the oil industry.

George W. Bush (1946–) was president from 2001 to 2009. See his Mini-Bio on page 90.

ILLEGAL IMMIGRATION

An estimated 1.4 million immigrants in Texas did not enter the state legally. Many undocumented workers do not pay taxes on their earnings in Texas—taxes that pay for schools, roads, police, hospitals, and other public services. On the other hand, undocumented workers work hard and their labor contributes to the economy. Texans have long debated how to deal with the issue of undocumented workers coming to their state.

"If we do nothing, in 10 years, just based on the current birth rate, we're going to have 50 million [**undocumented** workers and their children] in the United States," says state representative Leo Berman of Tyler. He fears they will drain state resources. But many undocumented workers do jobs for salaries that few Americans will accept. A housekeeper in South Texas who came to the United States illegally says, "I came here for the better opportunities, a better life and a chance for my family to do better than living in Mexico."

Sources: *Houston Chronicle*, January 4, 2007; ABC News KIII TV3, November 1, 2007

WORD TO KNOW

undocumented *lacking documents required for legal immigration or residence*

LOCAL GOVERNMENT

As in many other states, local government in Texas plays a key role. Throughout 254 counties, there are courts, sheriffs, town offices, and other government organizations. Within each county, elected officials include judges, attorneys, clerks, treasurers, and tax collectors.

Texas counties are big and small, ranging from fewer than 100 people to more than 3 million! The governments in each county build and maintain roads, airports, and parks. They hold elections, and they provide health and social services to needy residents.

Texas Counties

This map shows the 254 counties in Texas. Austin, the state capital, is indicated with a star.

NEW MEXICO

OKLAHOMA

ARKANSAS

LOUISIANA

MEXICO

GULF OF MEXICO

Red

Rio Grande

MEXICO

Dallas

Austin

Houston

N W E S

0   100 Miles
0   100 Kilometers

County boundary

1. ANDERSON	27. BURNET	53. CROCKETT	79. FORT BEND
2. ANDREWS	28. CALDWELL	54. CROSBY	80. FRANKLIN
3. ANGELINA	29. CALHOUN	55. CULBERSON	81. FREESTONE
4. ARANSAS	30. CALLAHAN	56. DALLAM	82. FRIO
5. ARCHER	31. CAMERON	57. DALLAS	83. GAINES
6. ARMSTRONG	32. CAMP	58. DAWSON	84. GALVESTON
7. ATASCOSA	33. CARSON	59. DEAF SMITH	85. GARZA
8. AUSTIN	34. CASS	60. DELTA	86. GILLESPIE
9. BAILEY	35. CASTRO	61. DENTON	87. GLASSCOCK
10. BANDERA	36. CHAMBERS	62. DEWITT	88. GOLIAD
11. BASTROP	37. CHEROKEE	63. DICKENS	89. GONZALES
12. BAYLOR	38. CHILDRESS	64. DIMMIT	90. GRAY
13. BEE	39. CLAY	65. DONLEY	91. GRAYSON
14. BELL	40. COCHRAN	66. DUVAL	92. GREGG
15. BEXAR	41. COKE	67. EASTLAND	93. GRIMES
16. BLANCO	42. COLEMAN	68. ECTOR	94. GUADALUPE
17. BORDEN	43. COLLIN	69. EDWARDS	95. HALE
18. BOSQUE	44. COLLINGSWORTH	70. ELLIS	96. HALL
19. BOWIE	45. COLORADO	71. EL PASO	97. HAMILTON
20. BRAZORIA	46. COMAL	72. ERATH	98. HANSFORD
21. BRAZOS	47. COMANCHE	73. FALLS	99. HARDEMAN
22. BREWSTER	48. CONCHO	74. FANNIN	100. HARDIN
23. BRISCOE	49. COOKE	75. FAYETTE	101. HARRIS
24. BROOKS	50. CORYELL	76. FISHER	102. HARRISON
25. BROWN	51. COTTLE	77. FLOYD	103. HARTLEY
26. BURLESON	52. CRANE	78. FOARD	104. HASKELL

105. HAYS	131. KENEDY	157. MASON	183. PANOLA
106. HEMPHILL	132. KENT	158. MATAGORDA	184. PARKER
107. HENDERSON	133. KERR	159. MAVERICK	185. PARMER
108. HIDALGO	134. KIMBLE	160. MCCULLOCH	186. PECOS
109. HILL	135. KING	161. MCLENNAN	187. POLK
110. HOCKLEY	136. KINNEY	162. MCMULLEN	188. POTTER
111. HOOD	137. KLEBERG	163. MEDINA	189. PRESIDIO
112. HOPKINS	138. KNOX	164. MENARD	190. RAINS
113. HOUSTON	139. LAMAR	165. MIDLAND	191. RANDALL
114. HOWARD	140. LAMB	166. MILAM	192. REAGAN
115. HUDSPETH	141. LAMPASAS	167. MILLS	193. REAL
116. HUNT	142. LA SALLE	168. MITCHELL	194. RED RIVER
117. HUTCHINSON	143. LAVACA	169. MONTAGUE	195. REEVES
118. IRION	144. LEE	170. MONTGOMERY	196. REFUGIO
119. JACK	145. LEON	171. MOORE	197. ROBERTS
120. JACKSON	146. LIBERTY	172. MORRIS	198. ROBERTSON
121. JASPER	147. LIMESTONE	173. MOTLEY	199. ROCKWALL
122. JEFF DAVIS	148. LIPSCOMB	174. NACOGDOCHES	200. RUNNELS
123. JEFFERSON	149. LIVE OAK	175. NAVARRO	201. RUSK
124. JIM HOGG	150. LLANO	176. NEWTON	202. SABINE
125. JIM WELLS	151. LOVING	177. NOLAN	203. SAN AUGUSTINE
126. JOHNSON	152. LUBBOCK	178. NUECES	204. SAN JACINTO
127. JONES	153. LYNN	179. OCHILTREE	205. SAN PATRICIO
128. KARNES	154. MADISON	180. OLDHAM	206. SAN SABA
129. KAUFMAN	155. MARION	181. ORANGE	207. SCHLEICHER
130. KENDALL	156. MARTIN	182. PALO PINTO	208. SCURRY

209. SHACKELFORD	235. VICTORIA
210. SHELBY	236. WALKER
211. SHERMAN	237. WALLER
212. SMITH	238. WARD
213. SOMERVELL	239. WASHINGTON
214. STARR	240. WEBB
215. STEPHENS	241. WHARTON
216. STERLING	242. WHEELER
217. STONEWALL	243. WICHITA
218. SUTTON	244. WILBARGER
219. SWISHER	245. WILLACY
220. TARRANT	246. WILLIAMSON
221. TAYLOR	247. WILSON
222. TERRELL	248. WINKLER
223. TERRY	249. WISE
224. THROCKMORTON	250. WOOD
225. TITUS	251. YOAKUM
226. TOM GREEN	252. YOUNG
227. TRAVIS	253. ZAPATA
228. TRINITY	254. ZAVALA
229. TYLER	
230. UPSHUR	
231. UPTON	
232. UVALDE	
233. VAL VERDE	
234. VAN ZANDT	

State Flag

Texas is called the Lone Star State because of the single star on its flag. No one knows who came up with the flag's design, but it was the flag chosen when Texas became a republic. The red, white, and blue bars represent courage (red), liberty (white), and loyalty (blue). In the blue section is a five-pointed white star.

State Seal

The state seal of Texas is two-sided. The front, or obverse, has a single, five-pointed star that is surrounded by live oak and olive branches. Along the top are the words "The State of Texas." The back, or reverse, of the seal features the six flags that have flown over Texas. "Remember the Alamo" appears on the top of the reverse, and "Texas One and Indivisible" runs along the bottom. Texas adopted this seal in 1836.

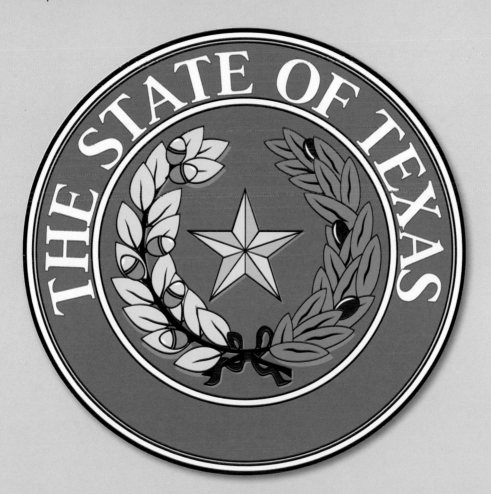

READ ABOUT

Workers attach a rudder to a freighter near the Houston Ship Channel.

CHAPTER EIGHT

ECONOMY

★

IF TEXAS WERE A NATION ON ITS OWN, ITS ECONOMY WOULD BE THE TENTH LARGEST IN THE WORLD. Texas grows, produces, and sells more products than South Korea, Brazil, India, or Russia. In the United States, its economy ranks second behind California, but Texas is catching up quickly.

A medical technician in Houston

WORKING IN TEXAS

Texas is home to 11 million workers, the second-largest total of any state in the nation. The two major economic centers in the state are Dallas and Houston. Dallas is a financial and technology center, and Houston is the site of many chemical and research companies.

In rural Texas—and there's plenty of rural Texas—agriculture dominates the economy. Cattle ranches and feedlots, fields of hay or wheat, and sweet-smelling citrus orchards are only part of the multibillion-dollar Texas farming industry. With so much money on the line, farmers must take advantage of science, technology, and marketing to make a profit.

FARMING AND AGRICULTURE

Raising cattle is a big moneymaker in Texas. Every year, ranchers sell nearly $6 billion worth of cattle and calves. People used to raise cattle on massive ranches, but that has changed. Now, many small cattle ranches raise only a few dozen head of cattle at a time. They then send them to central feedlots to be fattened up.

Texas ranks first in the United States in raising sheep and lambs. Not surprisingly, the state is also first in producing wool—the fleece sheared from the sheep each spring. Millions of bales of cotton from Texas make their way to textile mills and end up as jeans or bedsheets or tablecloths.

Grains dominate among Texas's cash crops. Texas is first in the nation in producing hay and second in producing sorghum grain. Texas farmers also grow 7 million bushels of oats yearly for horse feed and cereal. Texas corn becomes cattle feed, corn syrup, and popcorn.

FAQ

Q: WHERE DOES MOHAIR COME FROM?

A: Mohair is the hair of angora goats, which were first brought to Texas in the 1850s.

Workers harvesting honeydew melons in the Rio Grande Valley

Texas produces everything a family might need for a meal: broiler chickens, rice, cabbage, and onions for dinner, milk to drink, and watermelon for dessert. The state also has a large citrus fruit industry. The oranges generally end up as juice.

MANUFACTURING INDUSTRY

Since the late 1990s, Texas's manufacturing production has increased dramatically. The state produced $126.8 billion in manufactured goods in 2005, which is just over 8 percent of all manufacturing in the United States. Texas exports more manufactured goods than any other state. Manufacturing has grown for several reasons. The state has low taxes. Low costs of land and construction make building inexpensive. Also, Texas has a fast-growing labor market.

The state is also centrally located in North America and has ready sources of transportation—highways, railroad lines, air transportation, and

Top Products

Agriculture cattle, broilers, sheep and lambs, cotton, corn, sorghum, wheat, hay, cabbage, citrus fruit, peanuts, pecans, rice, watermelons, wool, and mohair

Manufacturing computers and electronics, industrial machinery, transportation equipment, chemicals, food manufacturing, furniture and wood products, military and aerospace products

Mining petroleum, coal

Fishing shrimps, oysters, clams, mussels, crabs, bass, catfish, drums, groupers

Major Agricultural and Mining Products

This map shows where Texas's major agricultural and mining products come from.
See a chicken? That means poultry is found there.

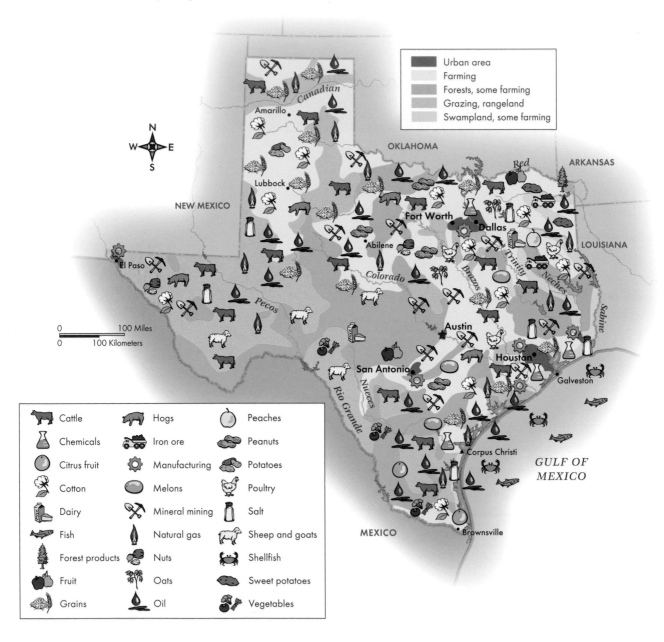

Legend:
- Urban area
- Farming
- Forests, some farming
- Grazing, rangeland
- Swampland, some farming

Key:
- Cattle
- Chemicals
- Citrus fruit
- Cotton
- Dairy
- Fish
- Forest products
- Fruit
- Grains
- Hogs
- Iron ore
- Manufacturing
- Melons
- Mineral mining
- Natural gas
- Nuts
- Oats
- Oil
- Peaches
- Peanuts
- Potatoes
- Poultry
- Salt
- Sheep and goats
- Shellfish
- Sweet potatoes
- Vegetables

0   100 Miles
0   100 Kilometers

seaports. Texas's location across the border from Mexico adds to the state's success as a manufacturing center. Along the border on the Mexican side, hundreds of maquiladoras—small factories—use cheap labor to produce materials and parts for assembly in Texas factories. The 1994 North American Free Trade Agreement (NAFTA) ended import taxes on parts made in Mexico that are assembled in Texas. Automakers are among the many to take advantage of NAFTA. Axles, wheels, seats, engine parts, lights, brakes, and other car parts are made in Mexico and shipped to plants in the United States, where workers put them together to make cars.

Texas ranks third in the nation in producing computers, computer parts, and other technology. Industry giant Texas Instruments was the first to produce a microchip, a common part in every mechanical device from spaceships to microwave ovens. Dell sells computers built to order over the Internet or by telephone.

Chemical manufacturing in Texas produces medicines, cosmetics, plastics, and petrochemicals—chemical products made from petroleum. Chemical export products include plastics, paint, soap, medicines, and fertilizer. Mary Kay Cosmetics, one of the largest cosmetics companies in the United States, is based in the Dallas suburb of Addison.

Oil companies, such as Chevron Phillips Chemical, E.I. du Pont de Nemours, and ExxonMobil, produce industrial plastics, fertilizers, and nylon.

MINI-BIO

MARY KAY ASH: PERFUME AND PINK CADILLACS

Hot Wells native Mary Kay Ash (1918–2001) founded the Mary Kay Cosmetics business with a $5,000 investment and a desire to help women in business. Ash believed in encouraging workers. Her top saleswomen won trips, jewelry, and pink Cadillacs. Working together, they turned Mary Kay Cosmetics into a billion-dollar business.

? Want to know more? See www.tshaonline.org/handbook/online/articles/MM/dhm1.html

THE ENRON SCANDAL

One of the worst corporate scandals in recent years involved Enron, an energy company based in Houston. It began in 1996, when executives at Enron stole company funds and created false records that inflated profits and hid debt. The top executives were charged with crimes, and it took years to bring them to justice.

The world's top oil companies, such as Texaco, ExxonMobil, Chevron, and Shell, have facilities in Texas. The oil industry refines gasoline for cars, diesel fuel for trucks, home-heating oil, and kerosene. The state processes about 360 million barrels of crude oil a year. That's one-fifth of the crude oil used in the United States.

Texas also yields coal, uranium, clay, sand and gravel, stone, salt, and talc. These mining operations employ nearly 150,000 people who produce $2.5 billion worth of these minerals a year. Texas coal fuels mainly electric utility plants and industrial operations.

The lumber industry in Texas has a 200-year history. Today, companies spend as much effort replanting forests as they do cutting trees down. In 1997, Texas ranked fifth in the country in private tree farms. Most of this wood is pine, which is used to make furniture and flooring.

What Do Texans Do?

This color-coded chart shows what industries Texans work in.

WOW

The first 7-Eleven store opened on a Dallas street corner in 1927. In 1967, 7-Elevens began selling Slurpee drinks.

%	Industry
19.3%	Educational, health, and social services, 1,779,801
12.0%	Retail trade, 1,108,004
11.8%	Manufacturing, 1,093,752
9.5%	Professional, scientific, management, administrative, and waste management services, 878,726
8.1%	Construction, 743,606
7.3%	Arts, entertainment, recreation, accommodation, and food services, 673,016
6.8%	Finance, insurance, real estate, rental, and leasing, 630,133
5.8%	Transportation, warehousing, and utilities, 535,568
5.2%	Other services (except public administration), 480,785
4.5%	Public administration, 417,100
3.9%	Wholesale trade, 362,928
3.1%	Information, 283,256
2.7%	Agriculture, forestry, fishing, hunting, and mining, 247,697

Source: U.S. Census Bureau, 2000

AEROSPACE

As Neil Armstrong prepared to leave the landing craft and become the first person to set foot on the moon in 1969, his first word was "Houston." Since 1962, rockets in the NASA space program have launched from Florida but been controlled from Houston.

The Johnson Space Center monitors missions. It also trains astronauts for their trips to space. The aerospace industry is not just the people who work in Mission Control. Aerospace workers build aircraft and engines, develop foods or products used by astronauts, and maintain equipment and facilities at the center.

One hundred ninety-seven businesses are directly connected to Texas's aerospace industry. These companies employ nearly 50,000 people and account for $8.5 billion in aerospace products.

SEE IT HERE!

JOHNSON SPACE CENTER

Have you ever dreamed of flying into space? Each year, nearly 1.5 million people visit the Lyndon B. Johnson Space Center in Houston to land a space shuttle, capture a satellite, or pull into the shuttle's storage bay—all in virtual reality. You can also see real spacecraft and watch IMAX movies of the stars and planets.

The first module of the *Apollo XI* spacecraft in Houston, March 1969

MINI-BIO

BERNARD HARRIS: SPACE DOC

Born and raised in Texas, Dr. Bernard Harris (1956–) used his medical knowledge in an unusual place—space. He logged 438 hours on the International Space Station and in Spacelab D-2 in the 1990s. He was the first African American to walk in space. After leaving NASA, Harris started a foundation that encourages children's interest in science.

❓ **Want to know more?** See www.jsc.nasa.gov/Bios/htmlbios/harris.html

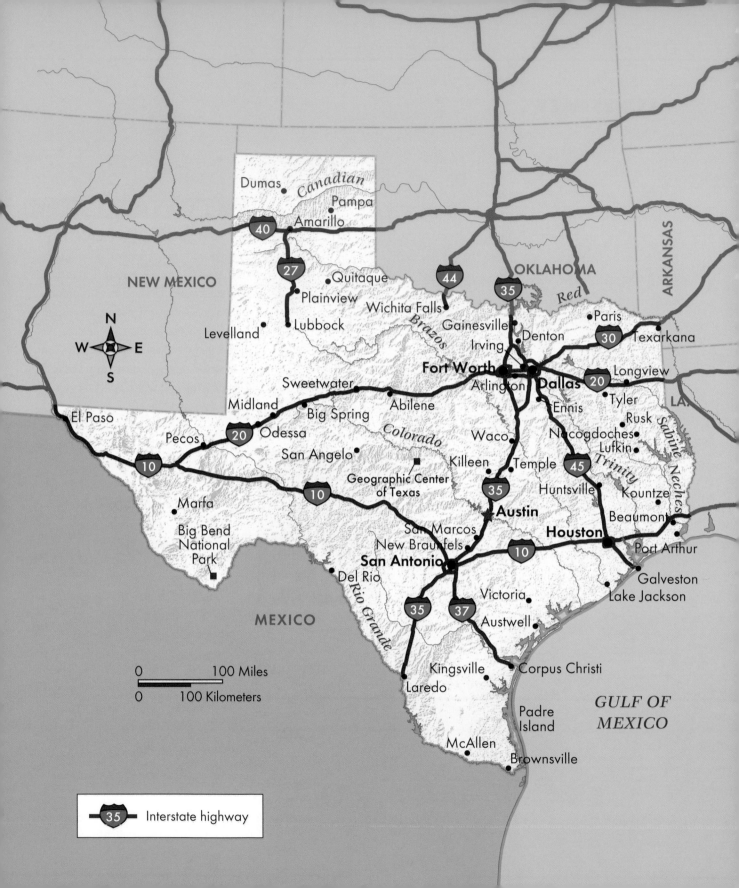

CHAPTER NINE

TRAVEL GUIDE

★

YOU KNOW THE HISTORY. You know the heritage. Now let's hit the road and see Texas firsthand. This is a long trip—Texas is a big state. We'll hit the beaches in the south, hike the mountains in the west, and check out some outrageous cars in the Panhandle. Along the way, we'll dance to conjunto, visit art museums, and tour the Johnson Space Center.

← Follow along with this travel map. We'll start in Dallas and travel all the way to Amarillo.

DALLAS/FORT WORTH

THINGS TO DO: Try on some cowboy boots, see Western art, or wander through a water maze.

Dallas

★ **Traders Village:** If you like flea markets, you'll love Traders Village. On any given weekend, you can buy everything from paper clips to parachutes, bulldozers to stuffed bison.

★ **The Science Place:** Catch a supersize IMAX movie and enjoy hands-on science exhibits. This is one place where the management says, "DO touch."

★ **Downtown Dallas Sculpture Tour:** Take a walk through downtown Dallas and see the more than 30 sculptures on display. They represent artists from the 19th century through modern times.

Cattle sculpture in Dallas

★ **Wild Bill's Western Store:** This store sells every possible type of Western gear—hats, boots, belts, buckles, and jeans.

★ **Morton H. Meyerson Symphony Center:** Called "The Mort," this music center is home to the Dallas Symphony Orchestra and also presents concerts throughout the year.

★ **African American Museum:** This museum covers all things African American—art, sports, history, theater, culture, and politics.

★ **Neiman Marcus:** For the person who has everything, Neiman Marcus department store offers some of the most unusual products in the world: mummy cases, matching his-and-hers camels, and diamond-studded underwear.

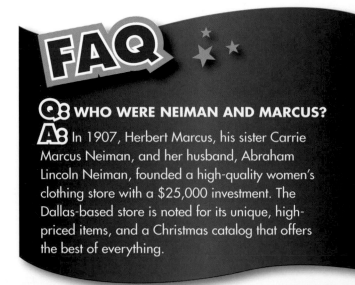

FAQ

Q: WHO WERE NEIMAN AND MARCUS?

A: In 1907, Herbert Marcus, his sister Carrie Marcus Neiman, and her husband, Abraham Lincoln Neiman, founded a high-quality women's clothing store with a $25,000 investment. The Dallas-based store is noted for its unique, high-priced items, and a Christmas catalog that offers the best of everything.

Fort Worth Water Gardens

Fort Worth

★ **Fort Worth Water Gardens:** This is not a garden. Rather, it is a maze of waterfalls and water sculptures that covers four city blocks. On a hot summer day, the water garden is really cool.

★ **National Cowgirl Museum and Hall of Fame:** This museum honors the women who rode 'em and roped 'em on the Texas range.

★ **Sid Richardson Collection of Western Art:** Frederic Remington and Charles Russell are just two of the Western-theme artists whose work is featured in this museum.

PINEY WOODS

THINGS TO DO: Climb a Native American burial mound, eat jambalaya, and have your picture taken next to the world's biggest fire hydrant.

Nacogdoches

★ **Caddoan Mounds State Historic Site:** In about 800 CE, Caddoans built a city centered on two temple mounds and a burial mound. Take a trip into Texas's earliest days and learn how early cultures lived.

Kountze

★ **Big Thicket National Preserve:** Big Thicket offers backpacking, hiking, fishing, horseback riding, hunting, kayaking, and nature walks.

Canoeing in Big Thicket National Preserve

Beaumont

★ **Texas Energy Museum:** How do geologists find oil? How did the oil form under the earth's surface? At this museum, a group of very intelligent robots tell you all about the oil industry and its history.

★ **Fire Museum of Texas:** At this museum, learn about fire safety, see antique firefighting equipment, and check out what may be the world's largest fire hydrant.

Port Arthur

★ **Cajun culture:** To get a taste of Cajun outside Louisiana, you just have to go to Port Arthur. There you can chow down on crawfish étouffée, jambalaya, and dirty rice. You'll also find yourself tapping your toes to the rhythms of zydeco music, played in clubs and on the street.

Rusk

★ **Texas State Railroad Historical Park:** All aboard! Find a seat. You are in for a treat—a train ride into history. The glorious days of train travel may be behind us, but this museum keeps the engines stoked and the rails humming with life.

GULF COAST

THINGS TO DO: Wiggle your toes in the sand, imagine riding a bucking bronco, and go eye-to-eye with a shark.

Houston

★ **Cockrell Butterfly Center:** Insect lovers—here's the place for you. At the Cockrell Butterfly Center at the Houston Museum of Natural Science, you can mingle with hundreds of live butterflies.

★ **Annual Livestock Show and Rodeo:** Held in the Astrodome, this livestock show and rodeo is the world's biggest. You can buy a bull, a goat, or a prized sheep. You can attend a pop or country-and-western concert. You can watch more than 450 professional cowboys wrestle steers, ride bulls, tame broncos, and rope calves.

The Houston Livestock Show and Rodeo is the world's largest event of its kind. In 2006, attendance approached 1.7 million people, with visitors from 52 countries.

Cheering the Astros at the Astrodome

★ **Houston Astros:** Play ball! Catch the Astros in action at the Astrodome.

Austwell

★ **Aransas National Wildlife Refuge:** More than 390 bird species make Aransas wetlands their winter home. This includes whooping cranes, roseate spoonbills, pelicans, ducks, herons, and egrets. On shore, javelinas, bobcats, and white-tailed deer avoid what look like logs but turn out to be alligators napping in the afternoon sun.

Corpus Christi

★ **Museum of Science and History:** This museum collects and preserves natural and cultural objects and offers educational exhibits, including a shipwreck, the Children's Wharf, and demonstrations about reptiles.

★ **Texas State Aquarium:** Tour the Living Shores exhibit, spend time with dolphins and some rather tricky otters, and travel down the Amazon in this modern aquarium. Watch out for the jellyfish—they sting!

★ **Padre Island National Seashore:** Bring a book, take a nap, collect seashells, wade in the water . . . but watch out for the mosquitoes.

Galveston

★ **Moody Gardens:** This 10-story structure re-creates life in a tropical rain forest, including the largest bat exhibit in the Southwest.

★ **Schlitterbahn Waterpark:** Surf's up! Bring your bathing suit and sunscreen to this water park, which features chutes, slides, and water coasters. It is covered and heated during winter months for year-round fun.

Schlitterbahn Waterpark

★ **George Ranch Historical Park:**
No trip to Texas is complete without a trip to a real cattle ranch and stock farm. This park is dedicated to cattle, cotton, and oil, and children get a hands-on taste of ranch life as it was in the 1830s.

Mardi Gras celebration in Galveston

SEE IT HERE!

MARDI GRAS—TEXAS STYLE

Although most Americans think of New Orleans when they think of Mardi Gras, more than a dozen Texas towns celebrate Mardi Gras, the traditional beginning of the Christian season of Lent. Parades, costumes, masks, music, and prizes keep the Cajun tradition of Mardi Gras alive in Texas.

HEADING WEST

THINGS TO DO: Buy traditional crafts, remember the Alamo, and enjoy Shakespeare under the stars.

Odessa

★ **The Southwest Shakespeare Festival:** Enjoy Shakespeare as the Elizabethans did, in a reproduction of the original Globe Theatre.

San Antonio

★ **Riverwalk:** This area along the San Antonio River combines shopping, dining, and San Antonio culture. Catch a show at the Aztec on the River, a grand movie palace where you can see silent films accompanied by live organ music.

★ **La Villita:** Working craftspeople make a visit to this community a must. Be sure to see the Old San Antonio exhibit of art and objects from San Antonio's history.

★ **Guadalupe Cultural Arts Center:** This center is dedicated to promoting Latino music, dance, literature, and other arts. It hosts film festivals, book fairs, and the Tejano Conjunto Music Festival.

The Alamo

★ **The Alamo:** The first stop every tourist makes in San Antonio is the Alamo. It is at the heart of Texas history, both as a mission under Spanish rule and as a fort in the fight for independence from Mexico.

★ **Natural Bridge Caverns:** See what can happen when moving water carves limestone.

El Paso

★ **Farmers Market:** From artichokes to art, persimmons to pottery, the farmers market offers the best produce and local artwork in El Paso. Open every Saturday morning from spring to late fall, this is an experience not to be missed.

★ **The Magoffin Homestead:** Here you can step into the past and learn about the hardships of frontier life, wagon trains, and the 19th-century wars. It is said that the spirits of El Paso pioneers still walk the halls of this real homestead.

Marfa

★ **Chinati Foundation:** Sculptor Donald Judd founded this contemporary art museum. Visitors come to gaze at abstract sculptures set in the West Texas landscape.

Big Bend

★ **Big Bend National Park:** Here you can enjoy the peaceful atmosphere of the Chisos Mountains and the Chihuahuan Desert. You might want to hike to a mountaintop or inspect the intricate beauty of a cactus.

Big Bend National Park

CENTRAL TEXAS AND THE PANHANDLE

THINGS TO DO: Watch more than 20 million bats head into the sky, walk through grasslands painted with Texas wildflowers, and learn more about hardworking horses.

Waco

★ **Dr Pepper Museum:** Here you'll find everything you ever wanted to know about Dr Pepper, how it was invented, and how it has made its mark on American pop culture.

★ **Texas Sports Hall of Fame:** Founded in 1951, this museum honors every great athlete Texas has ever turned out. Learn about Texas greats from the world of football, baseball, ice-skating, golf, tennis, track-and-field, and more.

★ **Lake Waco Wetlands:** Grab the binoculars and a beach chair and take some time to enjoy nature. This newly created park offers 130 types of birds and a plant nursery filled with aquatic plants.

Austin

★ **State Capitol:** Texas's state capitol is open to visitors most weekdays. When the legislature is in session, visitors can tour the galleries and watch lawmaking in action.

RATTLERS

Texas has ten rattlesnake species, found in the desert and the Hill Country. The sounds of the large and venomous diamondback, prairie, and eastern timber rattlesnakes strike fear in many Texans. Once a year, folks gather in Sweetwater for the Rattlesnake Roundup.

Former Dallas Cowboys quarterback Troy Aikman autographs a poster at the Texas Sports Hall of Fame.

★ **Lady Bird Johnson Wildflower Center:** Lady Bird Johnson—first lady while her husband, Lyndon B. Johnson, was president—dedicated herself to the conservation of Texas wildflowers. At the center, trails lead through gardens of plants native to Texas.

★ **Lyndon Baines Johnson Library and Museum:** Here you will find exhibits on politics, as well as objects and documents from Johnson's long political career.

★ **Congress Avenue Bridge:** The sun begins to set, and bats swoop out from beneath the Congress Avenue Bridge. Whether you like bats or not, it's a spectacular scene.

Lubbock

★ **Buddy Holly Center:** Celebrate the music of 1950s singer Buddy Holly, best remembered for the song "Peggy Sue."

Amarillo

★ **Route 66 Historic District:** This stretch of Route 66 features clubs, shops, restaurants, and the best burgers in town at the Golden Light Cafe.

★ **American Quarter Horse Heritage Center & Museum:** The quarter horse played a crucial role in the history of Texas ranches. This museum offers video presentations, live demonstrations, and interactive exhibits about this hardworking horse breed.

★ **Cadillac Ranch:** As art exhibits go, this one is a lulu. It features 10 graffiti-covered Cadillacs, partially buried in the ground. It's art, and it's unusual.

Cadillac Ranch

WRITING PROJECTS

Check out these ideas for creating campaign brochures and researching famous Texans. Or write you-are-there editorials!

118

ART PROJECTS

119

Create a great PowerPoint presentation, illustrate the state song, or research the state quarter and design your own.

TIMELINE

What happened when? This timeline highlights important events in the state's history—and shows what was happening throughout the United States at the same time.

122

FAST FACTS

Use this section to find fascinating facts about state symbols, land area and population statistics, weather, sports teams, and much more.

126

GLOSSARY

Remember the Words to Know from the chapters in this book? They're all collected here.

125

SCIENCE, TECHNOLOGY, & MATH PROJECTS

Make weather maps, graph population statistics, and research endangered species that live in the state.

120

PRIMARY VS. SECONDARY SOURCES

121

So what are primary and secondary sources? And what's the diff? This section explains all that and where you can find them.

BIOGRAPHICAL DICTIONARY

133

This at-a-glance guide highlights some of the state's most important and influential people. Visit this section and read about their contributions to the state, the country, and the world.

RESOURCES

Books, Web sites, DVDs, and more. Take a look at these additional sources for information about the state.

137

WRITING PROJECTS

★ ★ ★

Write a Memoir, Journal, or Editorial for Your School Newspaper!

Picture Yourself . . .

★ At a Juneteenth celebration. General Gordon Granger has arrived in Galveston to announce the end of slavery. Describe the joyful celebration.

SEE: Chapter Four, page 52.

GO TO: www.tsl.state.tx.us/ref/abouttx/juneteenth.html

★ Being in Texas at the time of the Texas Revolution. You are covering events inside the Alamo while General Santa Anna's troops amass outside. Describe the sights and sounds.

SEE: Chapter Three, pages 41–43.

GO TO: www.tshaonline.org/handbook/online/articles/AA/qea2.html

Create an Election Brochure or Web Site!

Run for office! In this book you've read about some issues that concern Texas today.

★ As a candidate for governor of Texas, create a campaign brochure or Web site.

★ Explain how you meet the qualifications to be governor, and talk about a few issues you'll focus on if you are elected.

★ Remember, you'll be responsible for Texas's budget! How would you spend the taxpayers' money?

SEE: Chapter Seven, pages 87–90.

GO TO: Texas's Government Web site at www.Texas.gov

Create an interview script with a famous person from Texas!

★ Research various famous Texans, such as Sam Houston, Bill Pickett, Quanah Parker, Ann Richards, Lance Armstrong, and many others.

★ Based on your research, pick one person you would most like to interview.

★ Write a script of the interview. What questions would you ask? How would this famous person answer? Create a question-and-answer format. You may want to supplement this writing project with a voice-recording dramatization of the interview.

SEE: Chapters Six and Seven, pages 68–95, and the Biographical Dictionary, page 133–136.

GO TO: The Handbook of Texas Online Web site at www.tshaonline.org/handbook/online. It has biographies of dozens of Texans.

Ann Richards

ART PROJECTS

★   ★   ★

Create a PowerPoint Presentation or Visitors' Guide

Welcome to Texas!

Texas is a great place to visit and to live! From its natural beauty to its bustling cities and historical sites, there's plenty to see and do. In your PowerPoint presentation or brochure, highlight 10 to 15 of Texas's wonderful landmarks. Be sure to include:

★ a map of the state showing where these sites are located

★ photos, illustrations, Web links, natural history facts, geographic stats, climate and weather, plants and wildlife, and recent discoveries

SEE: Chapter Nine, pages 106–115.

GO TO: The official Web site of the Texas Travel Industry Association at www.ttia.org. Download and print maps, photos, national landmark images, and vacation ideas for tourists.

Illustrate the Lyrics to the Texas State Song

("Texas, Our Texas")

Use markers, paints, photos, collages, colored pencils, or computer graphics to illustrate the lyrics to "Texas, Our Texas." Turn your illustrations into a picture book, or scan them into PowerPoint and add music.

SEE: The lyrics to "Texas, Our Texas" on page 128.

GO TO: The Texas state Web site at www.texas.gov to find out more about the origin of the state song.

Research Texas's State Quarter

From 1999 to 2008, the U.S. Mint introduced new quarters commemorating each of the 50 states in the order that they were admitted to the Union. Each state's quarter features a unique design on its reverse, or back.

Research and write an essay explaining:

★ the significance of each image

★ who designed the quarter

★ who chose the final design

Design your own Texas state quarter. What images would you choose for the reverse?

Make a poster showing the Texas quarter and label each image.

GO TO: www.usmint.gov/kids and find out what's featured on the back of the Texas quarter.

SCIENCE, TECHNOLOGY, & MATH PROJECTS

Graph Population Statistics!

★ Compare population statistics (such as ethnic background, birth, death, and literacy rates) in Texas counties or major cities.

★ In your graph or chart, look at population density and write sentences describing what the population statistics show; graph one set of population statistics and write a paragraph explaining what the graphs reveal.

SEE: Chapter Six, pages 70–74.

GO TO: Check out the official Web site for the U.S. Census Bureau at www.census.gov and at http://quickfacts.census.gov/qfd/states/48000. html, to find out more about population statistics, how they work, and what the statistics are for Texas.

Create a Weather Map of Texas!

Use your knowledge of Texas's geography to research and identify conditions that result in specific weather events. What is it about the geography of Texas that makes it vulnerable to things such as floods, hurricanes, tornadoes, and droughts? Create a weather map or poster that shows the weather patterns over the state, or display wet and dry years between 1895 and the present. Include a caption explaining the technology used to measure such weather phenomena, and provide data.

SEE: Chapter One, pages 16–17.

GO TO: National Oceanic and Atmospheric Administration's National Weather Service Web site at www.weather.gov for weather maps and forecasts for Texas.

Black-footed ferret

Track Endangered Species

Using your knowledge of Texas's wildlife, research what animals and plants are endangered or threatened.

★ Find out what the state is doing to protect these species.

★ Chart known populations of the animals and plants, and report on changes in certain geographic areas.

SEE: Chapter One, pages 18–20.

GO TO: Web sites such as www.tpwd.state. tx.us/huntwild/wild/species/?c=endangered

PRIMARY VS. SECONDARY SOURCES

★ ★ ★

What's the Diff?

Your teacher may require at least one or two primary sources and one or two secondary sources for your assignment. So, what's the difference between the two?

★ **Primary sources are original.** You are reading the actual words of someone's diary, journal, letter, autobiography, or interview. Primary sources can also be photographs, maps, prints, cartoons, news/film footage, posters, first-person newspaper articles, drawings, musical scores, and recordings. By the way, when you conduct a survey, interview someone, shoot a video, or take photographs to include in a project, you are creating primary sources!

★ **Secondary sources are what you find in encyclopedias, textbooks, articles, biographies, and almanacs.** These are written by a person or group of people who tell about something that happened to someone else. Secondary sources also recount what another person said or did. This book is an example of a secondary source.

Now that you know what primary sources are—where can you find them?

★ **Your school or local library:** Check the library catalog for collections of original writings, government documents, musical scores, and so on. Some of this material may be stored on microfilm. The Library of Congress Web site (www.loc.gov) is an excellent online resource for primary source materials.

★ **Historical societies:** These organizations keep historical documents, photographs, and other materials. Staff members can help you find what you are looking for. History museums are also great places to see primary sources firsthand.

★ **The Internet:** There are lots of sites that have primary sources you can download and use in a project or assignment.

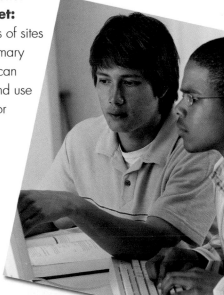

TIMELINE

★ ★ ★

U.S. Events

`9000 BCE`

Texas Events

Rock art at Seminole Canyon State Historical Park

c. 9000 BCE
Humans arrive in what is now Texas.

c. 3000 BCE
People along the Pecos begin making rock art.

`800 CE`

c. 800 CE
Mound Builders begin creating large ceremonial mounds.

`1500`

1528
Álvar Núñez Cabeza de Vaca is shipwrecked in Texas.

1540–1542
Francisco Vásquez de Coronado leads an expedition to Texas.

1565
Spanish admiral Pedro Menéndez de Avilés founds St. Augustine, Florida, the oldest continuously occupied European settlement in the continental United States.

`1600`

1607
The first permanent English settlement is established in North America at Jamestown.

1619
The first African indentured laborers in English North America are purchased for work in the Jamestown settlement.

Francisco Vásquez de Coronado's expedition

U.S. Events	Texas Events
1682	**1682**
René-Robert Cavelier, Sieur de La Salle, claims more than 1 million square miles (2.6 million sq km) of territory in the Mississippi River basin for France, naming it Louisiana.	The first Texas mission is built.

1700

1776
Thirteen American colonies declare their independence from Great Britain.

Stephen F. Austin

1787
The U.S. Constitution is written.

1800

1803
The Louisiana Purchase almost doubles the size of the United States.

1812–15
The United States and Great Britain fight the War of 1812.

1822
Stephen F. Austin establishes the first Anglo-American colony in Texas.

1830
The Indian Removal Act forces eastern Native American groups to relocate west of the Mississippi River.

1835
The Texas Revolution begins.

1836
The Republic of Texas is formed.

1845
Texas becomes a U.S. state.

1846–48
The United States fights a war with Mexico over western territories in the Mexican War.

1861–65
The American Civil War is fought between the Northern Union and the Southern Confederacy; it ends with the surrender of the Confederate army, led by General Robert E. Lee.

1861
Texas joins the Confederate States of America.

1867
Cowhands begin moving cattle along the Chisholm Trail.

124

U.S. Events

1898

The United States gains control of Cuba, Puerto Rico, the Philippines, and Guam after defeating Spain in the Spanish-American War.

1900

1917–18

The United States engages in World War I.

1929

The stock market crashes, plunging the United States more deeply into the Great Depression.

1941–45

The United States engages in World War II.

1954

The U.S. Supreme Court prohibits segregation of public schools in the *Brown v. Board of Education* ruling.

1964–73

The United States engages in the Vietnam War.

Sandra Day O'Connor

2001

Terrorists hijack four U.S. aircraft and crash them into the World Trade Center in New York City, the Pentagon in Arlington, Virginia, and a Pennsylvania field, killing thousands.

2003

The United States and coalition forces invade Iraq.

Texas Events

1892

The boll weevil begins moving into Texas, destroying cotton crops.

1901

Oil is discovered at Spindletop.

1925

"Ma" Ferguson becomes Texas's first female governor.

1941–1945

Texans fight in World War II.

1963

President John F. Kennedy is assassinated in Dallas.

1964

President Lyndon Johnson signs the Civil Rights Act.

1981

Sandra Day O'Connor becomes the first female U.S. Supreme Court associate justice.

1996

The Enron scandal starts to unfold in Texas.

2000

2001

Former governor George W. Bush becomes president.

2007

The San Antonio Spurs win the NBA championship

GLOSSARY

★ ★ ★

annexing uniting; incorporating territory into a country

archaeologists people who study the remains of past human societies

barrier islands islands that are created by the gradual buildup of sand and stones from the ocean floor

bigoted having unfair opinions of a group, based on that group's religion, race, or other factors

cavalry soldiers who ride on horseback

civil rights basic rights that are guaranteed to all Americans under the U.S. Constitution

endangered in danger of becoming extinct

expedition a trip for the purpose of exploration

foster care a government-run system of housing and caring for neglected or orphaned children

javelinas wild, piglike creatures with razor-sharp tusks

marketing the business of presenting products and services for sale to potential customers

missions places created by a religious group to spread its beliefs

obsidian jet-black volcanic glass

pictographs pictures drawn on rocks or cave walls

plantations large farms that grow mainly one crop

precipitation all water that falls to the earth, including rain, sleet, hail, snow, dew, fog, or mist

probation a time during which a person convicted of a crime is evaluated

reservoirs artificial lakes or tanks created for water storage

revenue taxes and other income collected by a government

sediment material eroded from rocks and deposited elsewhere by wind, water, or glaciers

segregation separation from others, according to race, class, ethnic group, religion, or other factors

shrapnel bomb, mine, or shell fragments

stocks shares in the ownership of a company

undocumented lacking documents required for legal immigration or residence

FAST FACTS

★ ★ ★

State Symbols

State seal

Statehood date	December 29, 1845, the 28th state
Origin of state name	From the word *tejas* used by the Hasinai and other Native peoples, meaning "all who are friends"
State capital	Austin
State nickname	Lone Star State
State motto	"Friendship"
State bird	Mockingbird
State flower	Bluebonnet
State gem	Topaz
State stone	Petrified palmwood
State song	"Texas, Our Texas" (see lyrics on page 128)
State tree	Pecan
State fair	Late September through mid-October at Dallas

Geography

Total area; rank	268,581 square miles (695,625 sq km); 2nd
Land; rank	261,797 square miles (678,054 sq km); 2nd
Water; rank	6,784 square miles (17,571 sq km); 9th
Inland water; rank	5,056 square miles (13,095 sq km); 2nd
Coastal water; rank	404 square miles (1,046 sq km); 13th
Territorial water; rank	1,324 square miles (3,429 sq km); 7th
Geographic center	McCulloch, 15 miles (24 km) northeast of Brady
Latitude	36° to 46° N
Longitude	94° to 106° W
Highest point	Guadalupe Peak, 8,749 feet (2,667 m)
Lowest point	Sea level along the Gulf of Mexico
Largest city	Houston
Number of counties	254
Longest river	Rio Grande, 1,240 miles (1,996 km)

Population

Population; rank (2006 estimate)	23,507,783; 2nd
Density (2006 estimate)	90 persons per square mile (35 per sq km)
Population distribution (2004 census)	82% urban, 18% rural
Ethnic distribution (2004 estimate)	White persons: 83.2%*
	Black persons: 11.7%*
	Asian persons: 3.3%*
	American Indian and Alaska Native persons: 0.7%*
	Native Hawaiian and Other Pacific Islanders: 0.1%*
	Persons reporting two or more races: 1.1%
	Persons of Hispanic or Latino origin: 35.1%†
	White persons not Hispanic: 49.2%

* Hispanics may be of any race, so they are also included in applicable race categories.
† Includes persons reporting only one race.

Weather

Record high temperature	120°F (49°C) at Seymour on August 12, 1936, and at Monahans on June 28, 1994
Record low temperature	−23°F (−31°C) at Julia on February 12, 1899, and at Seminole on February 8, 1933
Average July temperature	85°F (29°C)
Average January temperature	44°F (7°C)
Average annual precipitation	34 inches (86 cm)

State flag

STATE SONG

★ ★ ★

"Texas, Our Texas"

After a statewide contest, Texas legislators voted to adopt the song in 1929. The words are by Gladys Y. Wright and William J. Marsh, and the music is by William J. Marsh.

Texas, Our Texas! All hail the mighty State.
Texas, Our Texas! So wonderful, so great.
Boldest and grandest, withstanding ev'ry test
O Empire wide and glorious, you stand supremely blest.

Chorus:
God bless you Texas. And keep you brave and strong,
That you may grow in power and worth, throughout the ages long.
God bless you Texas. And keep you brave and strong,
That you may grow in power and worth, throughout the ages long.

Texas, O Texas! Your freeborn single star,
Sends out its radiance to nations near and far,
Emblem of Freedom. It set our hearts aglow,
With thoughts of San Jacinto and glorious Alamo.
(Chorus)
Texas, dear Texas! From tyrant grip now free,
Shines forth in splendor, your star of destiny.
Mother of heroes, we come your children true,
Proclaiming our allegiance, our faith, our love for you.
(Chorus)

NATURAL AREAS AND HISTORIC SITES

★ ★ ★

National Parks

Big Bend National Park sits on the Rio Grande right at the river's bend in West Texas. Its landscapes range from desert to mountain.

Guadalupe Mountains National Park includes the highest peak in Texas, canyons, and a large number of fossils.

National Monument

At *Alibates Flint Quarries National Monument*, visitors can see large pits in the flint rock made by ancient settlers.

National Recreation Areas

Amistad National Recreation Area, on the Mexico–United States border, boasts huge limestone cliffs. Tourists can also see rock art and parts of tools left by 300 generations of hunter-gatherers.

Lake Meredith National Recreation Area was formed when the Sanford Dam was built in the Texas Panhandle. More than a million visitors per year come to see the vistas and plant life of the High Plains.

National Preserve

Big Thicket National Preserve was formed to protect the region where the prairies, hardwood forests, wetlands, and deserts come together.

National Memorial

Chamizal National Memorial honors the 1963 treaty between the United States and Mexico, which ended a 100-year border dispute.

National Historical Parks

Lyndon B. Johnson National Historical Park honors the 36th president of the United States. Visitors can follow Johnson's ancestry and boyhood, learn about his achievements, and see his grave site.

San Antonio Missions National Historical Park is the site of four missions—San Juan, Concepción, San José, and Espada—built during the Spanish colonization of Mexico and the Southwest.

National Historic Site

Fort Davis National Historic Site was an important military site in the late 1800s, when soldiers guarded travelers on the San Antonio–El Paso Road.

SPORTS TEAMS

★ ★ ★

NCAA Teams (Division I)

Baylor University *Bears*

Lamar University *Cardinals*

Prairie View A&M University *Panthers*

Rice University *Owls*

Sam Houston State University *Bearkats*

Southern Methodist University *Mustangs*

Southwest Texas State University *Bobcats*

Stephen F. Austin State University *Lumberjacks*

Texas A&M University *Aggies*

Texas Christian University *Horned Frogs*

Texas Southern University *Tigers*

Texas State University–San Marcos *Bobcats*

Texas Tech University *Red Raiders*

University of Houston *Cougars*

University of North Texas *Eagles*

University of Texas–Arlington *Mavericks*

University of Texas–Austin *Longhorns*

University of Texas–El Paso *Miners*

University of Texas–Pan American *Broncos*

University of Texas–San Antonio *Roadrunners*

PROFESSIONAL SPORTS TEAMS

★ ★ ★

Major League Baseball

Houston *Astros*

Texas *Rangers*

National Basketball Association

San Antonio *Spurs*

Dallas *Mavericks*

Houston *Rockets*

National Football League

Dallas *Cowboys*

Houston *Texans*

National Hockey League

Dallas *Stars*

Women's National Basketball Association

Houston *Comets*

San Antonio *Silver Stars*

Major League Soccer

FC Dallas

Houston *Dynamo*

CULTURAL INSTITUTIONS

Libraries

The Center for American History is part of The University of Texas at Austin. It features map, book, and photograph collections of historical importance.

Daughters of the Republic of Texas Library in San Antonio is part of the Alamo. It contains materials on Texas history.

Mary Evelyn Blagg-Huey Library in Denton, part of the Texas Women's University Library system, contains an extensive collection of material about women.

Texas State Library and Archives Commission in Austin contains historical records on the history of the state along with genealogical collections and the state archives.

Museums

The Bob Bullock Texas State History Museum (Austin) features interactive stations that explore many significant events in the history of Texas.

East Texas Oil Museum (Kilgore) re-creates an oil boomtown of the 1930s. Exhibits include mementos of the area's early oil industry and a study of oil formations within the earth.

International Museum of Cultures (Dallas) highlights cultures from around the world.

Kimball Art Museum (Fort Worth) houses a stunning collection of art.

McAllen International Museum (McAllen) holds one of the country's largest collections of Latin American folk art.

Museo Alameda (San Antonio) tells the story of the Latino experience in America.

Panhandle–Plains Historical Museum (Canyon) keeps the history of northwest Texas alive.

Texas Natural Science Center (Austin) has displays featuring Texas botany, geology, history, and zoology.

Performing Arts

Texas has four opera companies, six symphony orchestras, five dance companies, and two professional theater companies.

Universities and Colleges

In 2006, Texas had 109 public and 100 private institutions of higher learning.

ANNUAL EVENTS

January–March

Southwestern Exposition and Livestock Show and Rodeo in Fort Worth (January or February)

Texas Citrus Festival in Mission (January or February)

Charro Days Festival in Brownsville (February)

San Antonio Stock Show and Rodeo (February)

Dallas Video Festival (March)

Oysterfest in Fulton (March)

Texas Independence Day across the state (March 2)

April–June

Mardi Gras in Galveston and other cities (spring)

Fiesta San Antonio in San Antonio (April)

Texas Sand Sculpture Festival in Port Aransas (April)

Jefferson Historical Pilgrimage in Jefferson (April or May)

Buccaneer Days in Corpus Christi (April or May)

National Polka Festival in Ennis (May)

Cinco de Mayo in Austin and other cities (May 5)

Kerrville Folk Festival (late May and early June)

Cantaloupe Festival in Pecos (June)

Juneteenth in Galveston and other cities (June 19)

Scottish Festival and Highland Games in Arlington (June)

Watermelon Thump in Luling (June)

July–September

Shakespeare Festival in Odessa (summer)

Black-Eyed Pea Jamboree in Athens (July)

Texas Cowboy Reunion and Rodeo in Stamford (July)

National Championship Barbecue Cookoff in Meridian (August)

Texas Folklife Festival in San Antonio (August)

Diez y Seis, or Mexican Independence Day, in various cities (September 16)

Rice Festival in Winnie (September or October)

Texas State Fair in Dallas (late September through mid-October)

October–December

East Texas Yamboree in Gilmer (October)

Oktoberfest in Fredericksburg and other cities (October)

Texas Rose Festival in Tyler (October)

International Championship Chili Cookoff in Terlingua (November)

Wurstfest in New Braunfels (November)

Día de los Muertos, or Day of the Dead, in various cities (October 31–November 2)

Festival of the Lights in San Antonio (December)

BIOGRAPHICAL DICTIONARY

Alvin Ailey (1931–1989) was a dancer and choreographer who founded the world-renowned Alvin Ailey American Dance Theater. He was born in Rogers.

Lance Armstrong (1971–) is a retired professional cyclist. He won the Tour de France seven times. After surviving a bout with cancer, he became a leading spokesman for the fight to find a cure. Armstrong was born in Plano.

Mary Kay Ash See page 103.

Stephen Fuller Austin See page 39.

Ninia Lilla Baird (1869–1963) turned her reputation as a baker into a business in Fort Worth. She built a fortune from the Mrs. Baird's Bread Company.

Ernie Banks (1931–) played baseball with the Chicago Cubs for 19 years. He hit 512 home runs in his career, the most ever by a shortstop. The Hall of Famer was born in Dallas.

Buffalo Hump (?–1870) was a celebrated Comanche war chief. He led his warriors in a battle at San Antonio in 1840, as well as in raids on Victoria and Linnville.

George H. W. Bush See page 93.

George W. Bush See page 90.

Álvar Núñez Cabeza de Vaca See page 30.

Claire Lee Chennault (1893–1958) founded the Fighting Tigers, a group of pilots who volunteered to fight the Japanese the year before the United States officially declared war on Japan. He was from Commerce.

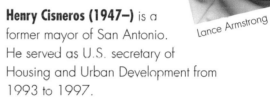

Lance Armstrong

Henry Cisneros (1947–) is a former mayor of San Antonio. He served as U.S. secretary of Housing and Urban Development from 1993 to 1997.

Sandra Cisneros See page 80.

Roger Clemens (1962–), a professional baseball player who last pitched for the New York Yankees, is a seven-time winner of the Cy Young award, five-time winner of the Sporting News Pitcher of the Year Award, and an 11-time All Star. In 2008, Clemens was accused of using illegal performance-enhancing drugs during his career. He denied the allegations. He has lived in Texas since 1977.

Bessie Coleman (1892–1926) was the first African American woman to become a licensed airplane pilot in the United States. Coleman, who traveled the country as a stunt pilot, grew up in Atlanta, Texas.

Juan Cortina See page 47.

Alvin Ailey

Walter Cronkite (1916–) anchored the *CBS Evening News* for 19 years. He is considered among the most respected news anchors in television. He grew up in Houston.

Robert Denard (1932–) developed DRAM, or Dynamic Random Access Memory, which is an important component in computer memories. He is from Terrell.

Sam Donaldson (1934–) is a popular news anchor for ABC News. He was born and raised in El Paso.

Jewel Frost Duncan (1902–1984) is a member of the Cowgirl Hall of Fame. She was one of two cowgirl calf ropers who competed against men in rodeos. She was from West Texas.

Dwight D. Eisenhower See page 93.

Miriam "Ma" Ferguson See page 61.

George Foreman (1949–) is a two-time world heavyweight boxing champion and Olympic gold medalist. Called "Big George," he is also a successful businessman and a Christian minister.

José Angel Gutiérrez See page 64.

George Foreman

Claudia "Lady Bird" Johnson

John Wesley Hardin (1853–1895) was an Old West outlaw and gunslinger. Born in Bonham, he was a cowboy on the Chisholm Trail in his early life and a lawyer later.

Bernard Harris See page 105.

Oveta Culp Hobby (1905–1995), born in Killeen, led the Women's Army Auxiliary Corps during World War II and later served in President Eisenhower's cabinet.

Buddy Holly (1936–1958), a native of Lubbock, was one of the most influential early rock-n-roll musicians. His songs include "Peggy Sue" and "That'll Be the Day."

Sam Houston See page 51.

Blind Lemon Jefferson (1893–1929) was a blues singer and guitarist, renowned for his wild, improvisational style, and was one of the first black singers to become widely successful. He was born in Couchman.

Claudia "Lady Bird" Johnson (1912–2007), born in Karnack, was the wife of President Lyndon B. Johnson. As first lady, she worked to beautify the nation's cities and highways. Later in life, she promoted the preservation and reintroduction of native plants in Texas.

Lyndon B. Johnson See page 93.

Michael Johnson (1967–), one of the world's fastest men, won five Olympic gold medals during his career. He is from Dallas.

Tommy Lee Jones (1946–), an actor from San Saba, has starred in many movies. He won an Academy Award for his role in *The Fugitive*.

Barbara Jordan See page 66.

Donald C. Judd (1928–1994) was a prominent American sculptor who began renting a house in Marfa in 1971. He later made Marfa his home and founded the Chinati Foundation, a contemporary art museum, there.

Henrietta King (1832–1925) and her husband, **Richard King (1824–1885)**, established the largest ranch in Texas, the famed King Ranch. Later in life, Henrietta became a prominent philanthropist.

Courtney Kupets (1986–) was the all-around world gymnastics champion in 2003 and 2004, and won a silver medal at the 2004 Olympics. She is from Bedford.

Tommy Lee Jones

Tara Lipinski

Tara Lipinski (1982–), who grew up in Sweetwater, won an Olympic gold medal in figure skating in 1998.

Willie Nelson (1933–) is a country singer and songwriter. He was born in Abbott.

Chester W. Nimitz (1885–1966) of Fredericksburg was a navy admiral. He led the Allied naval forces to victory against the Japanese in the Pacific during World War II.

Naomi Shihab Nye See page 81.

Sandra Day O'Connor See page 67.

Quanah Parker See page 57.

H. Ross Perot (1930–) is a billionaire who ran for president in 1992 and 1996. He hails from Texarkana and is one of the wealthiest people in America.

Bill Pickett See page 55.

Katherine Anne Porter (1890–1980) was a writer known for her talent with short stories. Born Callie Russell Porter in Indian Creek, she won the Pulitzer Prize and the National Book Award.

Robert Rauschenberg (1925–) is an acclaimed artist who combines painting and sculpture. His works include *Riding Bikes* and *Canyon*. He is from Port Arthur.

Ann W. Richards See page 89.

Gene Roddenberry (1921–1991) created the TV show *Star Trek*. Born in El Paso, he also wrote scripts for television programs such as *Dragnet*, *Naked City*, and *Have Gun–Will Travel*.

Nolan Ryan (1947–) was an eight-time Major League Baseball All-Star pitcher. He had 5,714 career strikeouts, the highest total in baseball history. He was born in Refugio and grew up in Houston.

Selena See page 79.

Sheryl Swoopes (1971–) plays for the Houston Comets in the Women's National Basketball Association. A native of Brownfield, she has been the league's Most Valuable Player three times and has won three Olympic gold medals.

Gene Roddenberry

William B. Travis (1809–1836) was a lawyer who joined the Texas army at the beginning of the Texas Revolution. He commanded the Texas forces at the Battle of the Alamo. He and all his men were killed in the battle.

Lee Trevino See page 83.

Victorio (ca. 1825–1880) was an important war chief among the Chiricahua Apaches. He led Apache raids into El Paso and Fort Davis.

Darold Williamson (1983–) of San Antonio is a track-and-field star who won a gold medal in the 2004 Olympic Games.

Bob Wills (1905–1975) was a country musician and leader of the Texas Playboys band. He was born near Kosse.

Beatrice Ximénez (1904–1989), a sculptor from Graytown, created what she called *animals feos* (ugly animals) using cement and metal rods. During her lifetime, she completed about 50 life-size animal figures.

Ralph Webster Yarborough See page 21.

"Babe" Didrikson Zaharias See page 82.

Lorenzo de Zavala See page 41.

Sheryl Swoopes

RESOURCES

BOOKS

Nonfiction

Alter, Judy. *Miriam "Ma" Ferguson: First Woman Governor of Texas.* Abilene, Tex.: State House Press, 2006.

Barenblat, Rachel. *Texas: The Lone Star State.* Milwaukee, Wis.: Gareth Stevens Publishing, 2002.

Gregson, Susan. *Sam Houston: Texas Hero.* Minneapolis: Compass Point Books, 2006.

Roza, Greg. *The Karankawa of Texas.* New York: PowerKids Press, 2005.

Tanaka, Shelley. *A Day That Changed America: The Alamo.* New York: Hyperion Press, 2003.

Wade, Mary Dodson. *Texas: Plants and Animals.* Chicago: Heinemann Library, 2003.

Warren, Betsy. *Wilderness Walkers: Naturalists in Early Texas.* Houston: Hendrick Long Publishing Company, 2000.

Fiction

Curry, Jane Louise. *Hold Up the Sky: And Other Native American Tales from Texas and the Southern Plains.* New York: Margaret K. McElderry, 2003.

Garland, Sherry. *A Line in the Sand: The Alamo Diary of Lucinda Lawrence, Gonzales, Texas 1836.* New York: Scholastic, 1998.

Gipson, Fred. *Old Yeller.* New York: HarperClassics, 1990.

Hale, Marian. *The Truth About Sparrows.* New York: Henry Holt & Company, 2004.

Janke, Katelan. *Survival in the Storm: The Dust Bowl Diary of Grace Edwards, Dalhart, Texas 1935.* New York: Scholastic, 2002.

Nye, Naomi Shihab. *Going Going.* New York: HarperTeen, 2005.

Paulsen, Gary. *Canyons.* New York: Bantam Doubleday Dell, 1991.

Sachar, Louis. *Holes.* New York: Yearling, 2003.

VIDEOS

The Alamo Documentary. Delta, 2004.
Biography: Davy Crockett. A&E Home Video, 2005.
Discoveries America: Texas. Bennett-Watt Entertainment, 2004.
Tour the Rio Grande Valley. Kirk Woodward, HHJM Video, 2001.

WEB SITES AND ORGANIZATIONS

The Alamo
www.thealamo.org
This official Web site of the Alamo offers a history of the historic mission and fort and lots of primary source material.

Aransas National Wildlife Refuge Complex
www.fws.gov/southwest/REFUGES/texas/aransas
Go to this site to learn more about whooping cranes and their summer home.

Big Bend National Park
www.big.bend.national-park.com/
Here is everything you ever wanted to know about Big Bend National Park.

State of Texas Web Site
www.state.tx.us
The official Web site for the state of Texas provides access to state and local government agencies.

Texas Legislature Online
www.capitol.state.tx.us/
At this site, you can read the Texas constitution, search Texas laws, and find out what state lawmakers are doing.

Texas Monthly
www.texasmonthly.com
This magazine covers life in contemporary Texas, reporting on people, politics, the environment, industry, and education.

Texas State Historical Association
www.tshaonline.org/handbook/online
This site offers links to information on important figures and events in Texas history.

Texas State Library and Archives Commission
www.tsl.state.tx.us
This site is home to the official archived history of Texas.

INDEX

★ ★ ★

AUTHOR'S TIPS AND
SOURCE NOTES

★ ★ ★

I began searching for resources for this book by asking the reference librarian at my local public library for help. She and I researched various topics concerning Texas and arranged to borrow books through the interlibrary loan services. Online resources were also helpful. The Handbook of Texas Online (www.tshaonline.org/handbook/online) provided both good information and a jumping-off point from which to do further research.

Working on this book required many trips to the library, a tour through Amazon.com, and endless hours searching the Internet. One of the most enjoyable books I read was Miroslav Sasek's *This Is Texas*.